THE ANTIPASTO TABLE

THE ANTIPASTO TABLE

MICHELE SCICOLONE

WILLIAM MORROW AND COMPANY, INC.

NEW YORK

The recipes for Bagna Caôda, Marinated Trout with Onions, Miniature Omelets with Cabbage and Leeks, Crisp Polenta Crostini with Porcini Mushroom Sauce, Mushroom and Parmigiano Salad, and Spinach and Rice Torte were originally commissioned for publication in *Food & Wine* magazine.

Library of Congress Cataloging-in-Publication Data

Scicolone, Michele.
    The antipasto table / Michele Scicolone.
      p.   cm.
    Includes bibliographical references (p.   ) and index.
    ISBN 0-688-10124-0
    1. Appetizers—Italy.   2. Cookery, Italian.   I. Title.
TX740.S327   1991
841.8'12—dc20   90-23395
                                                CIP

Printed in the United States of America

First Edition

1 2 3 4 5 6 7 8 9 10

BOOK DESIGN BY LINDA KOCUR

To my mom and dad,

Louise and Michael Scotto,

who taught me to appreciate good food,

and to my husband, Charles,

who helps me to enjoy it

CONTENTS

ACKNOWLEDGMENTS

Many people helped me in the writing of this book by sharing their knowledge and experience or by offering their opinions on my endless recipe testing.

Judith Weber encouraged me to develop the idea and guided me through the publishing process. My editor, Harriet Bell, was enthusiastic about the book from the start and helped me over many hurdles, big and small. Her organizational abilities really pulled it all together. Stephen Siller, as always, provided his advice and friendship. Judith Sutton and Paola De Kock read the manuscript carefully and corrected many inaccuracies. Linda Kocur developed the elegant design. Ann Disrude styled the jacket photograph and Jerry Simpson photographed it beautifully.

Special thanks to my husband, Charles, for collaborating on the wine notes. His constant encouragement, perceptive commentary, and passion for all things Italian has inspired me and made this work possible.

THE ANTIPASTO TABLE

INTRODUCTION

Some may argue that a dessert cart is more enticing, but I find an antipasto table harder to resist. Tender seafood, stuffed vegetables, moist mozzarella, and colorful salads spangled with herbs and glistening with golden-green olive oil are far more tempting to me than any sweets.

On my first trip to Rome twenty years ago, I regarded the bountiful antipasto tables in restaurants with suspicion. All those dishes couldn't be fresh, I reasoned. I assumed they were a collection of leftovers the chef was anxious to sell.

But closer inspection revealed that I could not have been more wrong. Everything was perfectly fresh. I noticed that most of the Italians in the restaurant were ordering, and enjoying, the *antipasto misto* (assorted antipasto), so I decided to try it, too.

It was so memorable that I still have the slightly smeared notes on what I ate: a tender white bean salad in a minty vinaigrette; a wedge of golden frittata stuffed with spinach and Parmigiano; miniature calamari tossed with herbs and lemon juice; a thin slice of *speck*; and a small tomato filled with herbed rice. Everything was so simple, fresh, and light, yet so good. The flavors were balanced with just the right degree of acid in the vinaigrette, a whiff of garlic in the calamari. Nothing was jarring, too hot or too cold, too bland or too spicy.

Since that time I have explored many an antipasto table, both at home and in Italy, and have filled many notebooks with recipes and ideas. I never fail to discover something new, either a variation on a familiar theme, a local specialty, or a new idea from an imaginative cook. I am constantly amazed by the spectacular variety and appeal of antipasti.

A tavola si sta sempre in allegria.

At the table one is always happy.

1

It is these recipes that you will find collected here along with many that have been handed down to me from Italian grandparents. Growing up in an Italian-American household meant that antipasto-style foods were a constant. My mother would scour the markets to find fresh vegetables at their peak season and stuff, bake, or sauté them in one of the many ways she had learned from her mother and my father's mother, both of whom were fine cooks. Sometimes she would prepare these foods early in the day, before it became too hot or she became involved in other tasks, for us to enjoy later for lunch or dinner. Others could be made days in advance, so she would prepare them in quantity to round out meals later in the week. This meant that there was always something good to eat on hand and meals were easy to put together.

In Italian, *pasto* means "meal" so *antipasto* means literally "before the meal." Historians believe that the antipasto concept is at least as old as ancient Rome, where meals usually began with small dishes of olives, shellfish, or salads, much as they do today. But antipasti are not mere appetizers. Very often, the same foods may be served as side dishes or a combination can comprise an entire meal. Antipasti can be made with fish, meat, cheese, vegetables, bread, legumes, and even fruit—in fact, just about anything that is good to eat.

Though there are no rules as to what is or is not an antipasto, they do have a number of common characteristics that make them well suited to the contemporary way of eating. For example, most antipasti are very easy to prepare. There are no complicated sauces, and cooking techniques are basic as can be.

Many antipasti require little or no cooking. Simple salads, cold meats, pickled vegetables, cheeses, and bread can be combined to make a splendid antipasto with very little effort and a minimum of time.

Antipasto flavors are intense and natural. Since only the choicest ingredients are used—ripe vegetables at their prime, sparkling fresh seafood, moist cured meats—a light dressing or marinade is all that's needed to enhance natural flavors.

Most antipasti are served at room temperature so that their flavors will not be dulled by extreme cold or heat. This means that they can be made in advance and they are perfect for all kinds of meals.

Antipasti are like beautiful, multicolored mosaics. The delicate pastels of the shellfish contrast with the vivid reds, greens, and yellows of the vegetables, pale pinks and burnished reds of the cured meats, creamy golden cheeses, and richly textured breads.

Antipasti are generally light and healthful because they are made with lots of vegetables, grains, and olive oil.

While dishes of many cuisines have some of these same characteristics, what makes antipasti distinctly Italian is reflected in the Italian art of eating. Italians can take very simple foods and put them together in such a way that the whole seems much greater than the sum of its parts. How they do it is no mystery, but an entirely different attitude toward food and eating.

In Italy, food is considered one of life's great pleasures. Meals are planned and discussed and are meant to be shared and savored with friends and family.

Not surprisingly, Italians also have a great deal of respect for their ingredients. Only the choicest foods are acceptable and they are eaten only when they are at their best and in season. This may mean no asparagus in September or peaches in January, but who would want to eat fruit or vegetables picked green in a foreign land, then shipped long distances so that they never quite ripen and are no more than a pale shadow of what they would be at their prime? Certainly not an Italian.

Tradition is important, too. Italian cooks steer away from creativity for the sake of creativity, preferring instead classic foods that need no explanation or apology and are always pleasing. This does not mean that the same dishes are repeated endlessly, but rather that new dishes are composed with care and sensitivity.

If one picture is worth a thousand words, then one look at an antipasto table can sum up the whole Italian philosophy toward food—the finest ingredients, simply prepared and eaten with joy.

ANTIPASTO MENUS

Antipasti can be as simple or as elaborate as you want them to be. One antipasto can be served at the beginning of a meal or an assortment can be the meal. A light lunch could consist of a frittata accompanied by a green bean salad. An important dinner might begin with one antipasto, such as Asparagus with Two Cheeses, followed by pasta, a meat or game course, and dessert. A brunch or dinner antipasto party for a group of friends or family could be made up of two or three cold vegetable antipasti, a rice salad, chicken salad, and a platter of cold meats and cheeses. Antipasti are adaptable to all kinds of meals and snacks and work well as appetizers, first or second courses, and side dishes.

In suggesting the number of servings per recipe in this book, I have assumed the meal will include two or three antipasti.

Antipasto Party on the Grill

Grilled Mozzarella and Dried Tomato Skewers
Grilled Vegetable Salad
Grilled Calamari Crests
Bruschetta
Wine: Frascati

Antipasto Brunch

Roasted Asparagus
Pepper and Potato Frittata

Sausage-Stuffed Tomatoes
Parmesan Bread
Wine: Valpolicella

Office Lunch-Hour Picnic for Two

Prosciutto and Melon
Marinated Mozzarella "Cherries"
Breadsticks
Wine: Orvieto

Buffet Supper for a Crowd

Olive Crostini
Seafood Salad with Pesto
Ligurian Chicken Salad
Raw Vegetables with Olive Oil
Tomato, Arugula, and Ricotta Salata Salad
Wine: Vernaccia di San Gimignano

Seafood Antipasto Dinner

Clams with Tomatoes and Capers
Seafood Rice Salad
Orange and Artichoke Salad
Semolina Focaccia
Wine: Pinot Grigio

No-Cook Saturday Lunch

Sliced Salami
Mozzarella with Parsley and Garlic
Hot Spiced Olives
Fresh Tomato Crostini
Wine: Galestro

Winter Antipasto Buffet

Bagna Caôda
Fennel with Parmesan Cheese

Veal-Stuffed Mushrooms
Marinated Carrots and Celery
Prosciutto Bread
Wine: Barbera

Summer Antipasto Menu

Chicken in Green Sauce
Eggplant and Pepper Terrine
Zucchini Carpaccio
Herbed Bruschetta
Wine: Chianti

Tailgate Antipasto Picnic

Prosciutto-Stuffed Focaccia
Marinated Mushrooms
Sicilian Eggplant Salad
Mozzarella with Parsley and Garlic
Wine: Dolcetto

After-Work Antipasto Dinner

Tuna and Vegetable Salad
Bean and Salami Salad
Breadsticks
Wine: Soave

Antipasto Cocktail Party

Parmesan with Dates
Asparagus with Prosciutto
Electric Cheese
Wild Mushroom Crostini
Olive and Rosemary Focaccia
Wine: Rubesco

THE ANTIPASTO PANTRY

No amount of expensive dressing or elaborate techniques can disguise foods made with poor-quality ingredients. Examine, smell, and, if at all possible, taste your ingredients before purchasing them or using them in a recipe. You will quickly learn to judge when they are at or past their prime and be able to make adjustments where necessary.

Certain ingredients appear regularly in antipasto recipes. If you keep a supply of them on hand, preparation will be even simpler.

Beans • FAGIOLI •

Perfectly cooked dried beans have a tender, creamy texture while retaining their shape. The Tuscan way to achieve this is to cook the beans slowly in the oven as described on page 74. Oven cooking insures that the beans cook evenly and the result is far superior to beans cooked on top of the stove.

Once cooked, the beans can be eaten with just a drizzle of olive oil and some black pepper or they can be kept in the refrigerator for up to three days to use in soups, salads, or other dishes.

Canned beans are a convenient substitute for home-cooked beans, though the flavor is sometimes lacking. Try several brands to determine which are the best. Rinsing canned beans helps to freshen their flavor. To do so, place them in a large strainer and run them under cool water before using.

Black Pepper • PEPE NERO •

Once black pepper is ground, the flavor quickly fades, so it is important to use only pepper that has been freshly ground in a mill. I have two pepper mills, one that grinds coarsely for when I want a more pronounced pepper flavor and texture, and one that grinds finely for when just a subtle peppery hint is needed.

Bread Crumbs • BRICIOLE DI PANE •

Bread crumbs are an essential ingredient in many of these recipes, but the bread crumbs available in cans are made from too-sweet white bread. Seasoned bread crumbs are dreadful and should not be used under any circumstances.

It is easy to make your own crumbs from scraps of leftover bread. Use only bread that is unflavored. Cut it into small pieces and place it in a turned-off oven with a pilot light, or in an electric oven at a very low temperature, until completely dry. Store the bread in a sealed container. When you have enough scraps, place them in a food processor or blender jar and grind them fine. Store in a tightly covered jar in the refrigerator until ready to use.

Capers • CAPPERI •

I had only a vague idea of what capers were until I went to Sicily. There, caper plants grow out of practically every stone wall. In June, the plants are in full bloom with gorgeous pink and white brushlike flowers, but it is not the flowers that are valued. The tiny unopened buds of these flowers are the capers. To gather them before the plants flower, the locals risk life and limb leaning over crumbling walls and fences with a long hooked wire. With this device, they can lift the stems high enough to gather the flower buds. The buds are then preserved in salt or, more commonly, in vinegar.

The tinier capers have an intense flavor and are considered more desirable. Larger capers can be finely chopped to release their flavor.

Garlic • AGLIO •

I become wary when I hear someone say, "I love garlic." I love garlic too, but all too often the philosophy is that if a little is good, more must be better and so two or three cloves are used where one would be plenty. The result is garlic overload and total indigestibility.

Raw garlic is very powerful and chopping, crushing, or slicing it releases its flavor. The more finely chopped, crushed, or pureed, the more pronounced the flavor will be.

Cooking garlic tames some of its pungency. For sautéing, garlic is best chopped or pressed. I prefer to place the garlic in the pan with the oil before heating the pan. This way, I can be sure that the garlic will not burn as it sometimes does when added to hot oil. The garlic should be sautéed just until its aroma is released by the heat. The color should be no darker than a very pale gold. Overcooked garlic that is dark brown or blackened tastes acrid and should be discarded. Garlic that is baked or cooked slowly in oil takes on a very mild, nutlike flavor and can be eaten like a vegetable.

Fresh garlic is milder than older garlic. Buy heads that are plump, not shriveled or bruised, and don't buy more than you can use within a reasonable amount of time, about two weeks. Keep garlic in a cool, dry place. I keep it in an open container in the refrigerator.

Never substitute dried garlic powder or preserved garlic in any form for fresh. It has a stale, sour flavor and aroma that is immediately detectable and has a nasty habit of leaving a lingering odor about the person who has eaten it.

H e r b s • ODORI •

Fresh herbs are easy to come by in Italy and are important ingredients in many antipasto recipes. Fortunately, they are becoming easier to find here too.

The two most important fresh herbs for antipasti are parsley and basil. Parsley adds vivid color and a clean, fresh flavor to all kinds of foods. The dark green flat-leaf variety often called Italian parsley is preferable to the curly-leaf variety since it is more intensely flavorful. Not only is parsley good on its own, it can also restore a measure of fresh flavor to dried herbs such as oregano or rosemary when they are used in combination.

Fresh parsley keeps well in the refrigerator for a week to ten days. Do not wash the leaves until you are ready to use them. Trim off the base of the stems and place the parsley in a jar with an inch or two of water. Invert a plastic bag over the jar and store it in the refrigerator. Change the water every day or two.

The sweet flavor and aroma of basil is a natural complement to tomatoes, eggs, and many other foods. Though it is a tender annual, it grows easily on a sunny windowsill. I always try to keep a few plants growing through the winter.

Controversy rages over whether basil should be snipped, chopped, or torn. I take no sides here and admit that I like basil no matter how it is cut. Chopped basil is good when I want the basil flavor to permeate the food. When I need to retain all of the flavor and moisture of the herb as in a salad or dressing, I am more likely to tear it into small pieces. When using basil as a garnish, I cut it with scissors into shreds and scatter the pieces over the finished dish. The difference is subtle but noticeable.

Many people like to freeze summer's fresh basil to have on hand in the colder months. I do not like the result, however, and would not recommend it. Fresh basil may be stored the same way as fresh parsley, though it will not last as long.

Dried parsley and basil are quite useless. Neither has a flavor that remotely resembles the fresh herb and they really have no place in good cooking of any kind.

Fresh oregano, rosemary, sage, and mint may be a bit harder to come by but are well worth seeking out. In their dried forms, these herbs can be quite pungent, so use them sparingly. Since it is not possible to remove the dried herb from finished dishes the way a sprig of a fresh herb can be removed, the flavor can seem too strong. There are times, however, when I prefer dried oregano or rosemary for their pronounced flavor, as in the Spicy Squid Salad on page 223. A general rule of thumb is to use one third the amount of dried herbs as fresh.

When you use dried herbs, be sure to smell and taste them before adding them to food, as their flavor can vary. If they are too old, they lose flavor or become musty. Decorative spice racks for storing dried herbs may look pretty, but dried herbs will last longer and taste better if they are stored in a cool, dark place.

Mozzarella

Though mozzarella is best known as pizza cheese, it has many other uses. If at all possible, buy fresh mozzarella, a soft and tender white cheese that is both imported from Italy and made domestically. Many Italian grocery stores in this country make their own mozzarella from fresh cow's milk daily. At least one company in the Northeast, Polly-O Dairy Products, makes a fresh mozzarella that is sold in plastic tubs in supermarkets.

In Italy, mozzarella may be made either from cow's milk or from all or part water buffalo milk and labeled *mozzarella di bufala*. Buffalo-milk mozzarella has a creamier texture and richer flavor than the cow's milk cheese and can be very good. It is sometimes imported here but it is more expensive than cow's milk mozzarella and very perishable, so if you find some, be sure that it is really fresh.

Many Italian food stores sell smoked mozzarella. The best of its kind is fresh cheese that has been smoked over a wood fire. It can be substituted for plain mozzarella in any recipe where a smoky flavor would be welcome.

Olive Oil • OLIO D'OLIVA •

At one point, I thought it might be necessary to change the title of this book to *The Olive Oil Cookbook* since it seemed that every recipe used that quintessential Italian ingredient.

I love the taste of olive oil and keep several varieties on hand for various cooking purposes. For example, I like a light-bodied extra-virgin oil for dressing delicate lettuce salads and many fish and shellfish preparations. I reserve a heavier-bodied and flavored extra-virgin oil for brushing over grilled vegetables, meats, and other substantial foods and as a condiment to drizzle over soups or pasta as a last-minute seasoning before serving. I generally do not use olive oil for frying because its flavor can be too pronounced, but when I do, I find that a pure grade of olive oil is satisfactory.

There is a lot of confusion about olive oil grades. Many people think that extra-virgin oil, the highest-quality grade, is oil extracted from the first cold pressing of olives. In fact, this may or may not be the case.

Cold pressing, that is, crushing the olives without heating them, yields better-quality oil than heat extraction methods. It is, however, labor intensive and not feasible for large-quantity producers. Since olive oil is now big business, it has become increasingly rare, though not impossible, to find processors that actually cold press their olives.

According to Italian law, the level of oleic acid in the oil is the main factor in determining an oil's grade. To be labeled extra-virgin, an oil must contain less than 1 percent oleic acid (some producers of quality oils insist on a level of less than 0.5 percent). It does not have to be cold pressed.

There are other grades of Italian oils according to their increasingly higher level of oleic acid. In addition to extra-virgin oil, the other grade that is most commonly available is "pure" olive oil, the kind found in supermarket tins. Pure oils are made from blends of oils that are treated to eliminate off flavors or high acidity. A small amount of extra-virgin oil is then blended in to provide flavor.

Several big oil manufacturers have recently come out with something called "extra-light" olive oil. I find the term somewhat misleading. Extra-light oil is nothing more than pure olive oil with less extra-virgin blended in, so that it is extra light in flavor, not calories. All olive oils, as well as all other vegetable oils, have the same number of calories.

Many countries produce olive oil and all have their own laws about labeling—which may or may not be similar to the Italian laws.

Choosing an olive oil is a matter of taste. Oils have different flavor and texture characteristics according to their region of origin, the type of olives used, the degree of ripeness of the olives when picked, and so forth. For example, Tuscan oils are peppery, grassy, and green while Ligurian oils are golden green, delicate, and light. Buy small bottles of several different brands and taste them before deciding on your favorites.

The Italians say, *"Il vino è buono quando e vecchio, l'olio se è nuovo"* —"Wine is good when it is old, oil when it is new." Olive oil should be used when it is fresh. Many, though not all, extra-virgin oils are vintage dated. Use them as soon as possible after purchasing and don't buy more than you can use within a reasonable amount of time. It is hard to give an exact time that olive oil will last because storage conditions have a tremendous influence on the quality. Keep olive oil in a cool, dark place as heat and light destroy the oil's flavor. If you have just opened a new bottle and are taking off for a month's vacation, by all means put it in the refrigerator. It will solidify from the cold, but will quickly liquify at room temperature.

Olive Paste • PASTA DI OLIVE •

Olive paste is a puree of olives that is available in jars at most Italian markets and in many supermarkets. Until recently, I had seen only black olive paste, but now I have discovered that there is a green olive paste too. Both are made from finely chopped olives, extra-virgin olive oil, herbs, and, sometimes, garlic and anchovies. Spread the rich paste on crostini, use it in a salad, or mix it with pasta. If you prefer, you can make your own olive paste in a food processor with the olives and seasonings of your choice (see Olive Crostini, page 145).

Olives • OLIVE •

The salty tang and richness of olives make them desirable both as an ingredient in a variety of dishes and an accompaniment to other foods. Brown, black, purple, or green, large or small, olives are an important part of an antipasto table. Whatever color, size, or shape you choose, olives should be full of flavor. Excellent olives are imported from France, Greece, Spain, and Italy. Two of my favorites are the large green Sicilian olives and the medium-size brownish-black Kalamata olives from Greece, and I always try to keep a container or two of these in the refrigerator for cooking or just snacking. Both are readily available and adaptable to many purposes. They keep indefinitely.

Use whichever varieties you prefer, but avoid canned ripe olives, which are tasteless.

To pit olives quickly, place them a few at a time on a cutting board. Lay the broad end of the flat side of the blade of a heavy chef's knife on top of the olives and rap the blade sharply with the heel of your hand. This should crack the olives open so that the pits can be removed easily.

Parmigiano-Reggiano

Parmigiano-Reggiano is surely Italy's finest and most famous cheese. Unfortunately, many poor excuses for cheese sold under the name of Parmesan bear no relationship to the real thing. For that reason, I prefer to use the name Parmigiano-Reggiano or, at least, Parmigiano, in my recipes so that it will serve as a reminder not to settle for anything less.

Authentic Parmigiano-Reggiano is a partially skimmed cow's milk cheese that can be made only in a limited area around the Italian city of Parma. It has a creamy straw-gold color and rich, nutty flavor, which make it ideal for eating as well as for cooking.

Parmigiano-Reggiano is made in large wheels that weigh about seventy pounds. Each one has the words "Parmigiano-Reggiano" imprinted into the rind as well as the year in which it was made. When buying a piece that has already been cut, look for the name on the rind. Never buy Parmigiano that has already been grated. You have no way of knowing what kind of cheese it really is and, besides, cheese dries out and loses its flavor rapidly after grating so it is essential to grate it only as needed.

In several of these recipes, Parmigiano is shaved into small paper-thin scale-like slices to be scattered over salads or carpaccio. Don't expect your cheese store to cut these pieces for you. Parmigiano is too firm to cut on a slicing machine—and besides, the slices are very thin and fragile and would surely crumble before you could get them home. To make these thin slices, take a chunk of cheese and use a swivel-bladed vegetable peeler to shave them off.

Pecorino Romano

Pecorino Romano is a sheep's milk cheese used by many Southern Italians. It is tangy, sharp, and salty and it can be very good in some dishes, particularly those flavored with tomatoes and garlic or in some bread-crumb stuffings. However, it should not be used as an alternative to Parmigiano except where indicated.

Pine Nuts • PIGNOLI •

Pignoli are the seeds of a certain variety of pine tree and are extracted from pine cones. They have a unique mild flavor and soft texture compared to the crispness of other nuts.

Like all nuts, pignoli taste best when lightly toasted. Bake them in a 350°F oven for 5 to 10 minutes, or until they turn a light beige color. The little bags and jars available in supermarkets are quite expensive but health food stores sell excellent pine nuts in bulk. Store them in the refrigerator or freezer to prevent them from turning rancid.

Salt • SALE •

I have not given measurements for salt in most recipes because I have found that tolerance and taste for salt varies considerably. Also, many ingredients used in antipasti are already salty and their degree of saltiness needs to be considered.

Coarse kosher or sea salt is preferable to ordinary table salt. Since they are manufactured without additives, kosher and sea salt have a pure flavor and no medicinal aftertaste. The level of saltiness can vary though, so always add salt to your taste.

Tomatoes • POMODORI •

My grandfather came from Italy and grew vegetables in his tiny garden behind his house in Brooklyn. I remember him taking me by the hand when I was not much taller than the tomato plants and showing me how to prune them so that they would produce more and better fruit. When the tomatoes were perfectly ripe, we would each pick one and eat it in the garden while the tomato was still warm from the sun.

A perfectly ripe, fresh tomato is a pure and simple delight. But out-of-season tomatoes are miserable things, really not worth eating, no matter how costly they are. Unfortunately, this is a lesson many of us have not yet learned.

Though there are many recipes in this book using fresh tomatoes, they are intended to be made only with excellent ripe tomatoes. In some cases, other varieties, such as plum or cherry tomatoes, which seem to have a longer season, can be substituted, or you can use dried tomatoes where appropriate. Canned imported Italian peeled tomatoes can be used in cooked tomato recipes.

When you do find good ripe tomatoes, don't ruin them by placing them in the refrigerator. Chilled tomatoes quickly get mushy and tasteless; keep them at room temperature until ready to use.

VEGETABLES

Le Verdure

No one knows as many ways to cook vegetables as Italians. Perhaps it is because they get so much inspiration from the plentiful assortment that always seems to be available in the markets. Large-leafed greens such as escarole, Swiss chard, and spinach, artichokes with their long stems and leaves still attached, many varieties of wild and cultivated mushrooms, and ripe, bursting tomatoes in almost every size and shape all tempt shoppers to go home and cook. And they do, using vegetables in an unending array of sauces, soups, main courses, side dishes, and antipasti. There are so many vegetable antipasti to choose from that it was hard to decide when to stop adding more vegetable recipes!

Mangia

poco, bene,

e spesso.

Eat little,

well,

and often.

STEWED BABY ARTICHOKES

Carciofini Stufati

Serves 8

Baby artichokes, half the size of the usual variety, are available for a brief period in the spring. They are sweeter and more tender than the large variety. If only large artichokes are available, trim them well and cut them into quarters or sixths.

Juice of 1 lemon
2 pounds baby artichokes
1 small onion, peeled and finely chopped
3 tablespoons extra-virgin olive oil
1 garlic clove, peeled and finely chopped
2 tablespoons chopped flat-leaf parsley
⅓ cup water
Salt and freshly ground black pepper

1. Fill a large bowl with cold water and add the lemon juice. Trim the artichokes by snapping off the outer leaves at the base, leaving just the central core of pale, tender leaves. Cut about ½ inch off the tops. With a small paring knife, trim the leaf ends from the base and peel off the tough outer layer of the stem. Cut the artichokes in half lengthwise. With a small knife, scrape out the fuzzy chokes at the core. As you finish each artichoke, drop it into the lemon water to prevent it from turning dark. Drain before cooking.
2. In a large saucepan, cook the onion in the olive oil over medium heat until tender, about 5 minutes.
3. Stir in the garlic and parsley and cook for 30 seconds more. Add the drained artichokes, water, and salt and pepper to taste.
4. Cover and cook over low heat until the artichokes are tender when pierced with a knife, about 15 minutes. Serve warm or at room temperature.

FRIED ARTICHOKE HEARTS

Fondi di Carciofi Fritti

Serves 8

Juice of 1 lemon
6 large artichokes
Salt
2 large eggs
½ cup freshly grated Parmigiano-Reggiano
Freshly ground black pepper
1 cup dry bread crumbs
Vegetable oil for frying
Lemon wedges

1. Fill a large bowl with cold water. Add the lemon juice. Trim the artichokes by snapping off the outer leaves at the base, leaving a central core of pale, tender leaves. Cut about 1 inch off the tops. With a small paring knife, trim the leaf ends from the base and strip off the tough outer layer from the stem. Cut off the stems ½ inch from the base and drop the artichokes into the lemon water to prevent them from turning dark. Drain before cooking.

2. Bring a large pot of lightly salted water to a boil. Add the drained artichokes, cover, and cook for 15 minutes. Drain and cool.

3. Halve the artichokes lengthwise and scoop out the fuzzy chokes. Cut each half lengthwise into quarters.

4. In a shallow dish, beat the eggs and cheese with salt and pepper to taste. Dip the artichoke pieces into the mixture and drain off the excess. Roll the artichokes in the bread crumbs. Place on a wire rack to dry for 15 to 30 minutes.

5. Fill a deep fryer with oil according to the manufacturer's recommendation or pour 1 inch of oil into a deep heavy skillet. Heat the oil to 375°F on a deep-frying thermometer. Add just enough of the artichoke pieces to make a single layer. Fry the artichokes, turning once, until golden, about 6 minutes.

6. Remove with a slotted spoon and drain on paper towels. Repeat with the remaining artichokes. Serve hot with the lemon wedges.

ASPARAGUS ROLLS WITH SALMON

Involtini di Salmone con Asparagi

Serves 6

Thick and thin asparagus are like two different vegetables. Thin asparagus is nice for salads and with pasta while the thick-as-a-thumb kind can take heavier sauces or wrappings such as this one and the variation below.

1 pound thick asparagus
Salt
¼ pound thinly sliced smoked salmon, cut into
** 2- × 1-inch strips**
¼ cup extra-virgin olive oil
1½ to 2 tablespoons fresh lemon juice
Freshly ground black pepper
1 tablespoon finely chopped flat-leaf parsley
1 hard-cooked egg yolk, finely chopped
Lemon slices

1. Soak the asparagus in cold water for 10 minutes. Trim off the tough lower portion of each stalk where the color changes from green to white.
2. In a large skillet, bring about 1 inch of water to a boil. Add the asparagus and salt to taste. Cook until the asparagus is tender, about 5 to 10 minutes, according to its thickness.
3. Drain and rinse under cold running water. Pat the asparagus dry with paper towels.
4. Roll a strip of salmon lengthwise around each asparagus spear. Arrange the asparagus on a serving platter.
5. In a small bowl, beat the oil, lemon juice, and salt and pepper to taste. Stir in the parsley. Pour the dressing over the asparagus and sprinkle with the chopped egg yolk. Garnish with the lemon slices.

Asparagus with Prosciutto Cut 4 ounces thinly sliced prosciutto in half crosswise. Prepare the asparagus through step 3 above. Wrap a piece of prosciutto around each spear. No sauce is needed.

ROASTED ASPARAGUS

Asparagi al Forno

Serves 6

Roasted asparagus turns lightly brown and crisp. The flavor is quite a change from steamed or boiled asparagus. The best part about preparing asparagus this way is that it doesn't have to be peeled.

1½ pounds thick asparagus
¼ cup extra-virgin olive oil
Salt and freshly ground black pepper

1. Preheat the oven to 400°F. Lightly oil a 13- × 9- × 2-inch baking pan.
2. Soak the asparagus in cold water for 10 minutes. Trim off the tough lower portion of the stalks where the color changes from green to white.
3. Place the asparagus in the pan and drizzle with olive oil. Sprinkle with salt and pepper to taste and toss well to coat. Arrange the asparagus in two layers with the tips of the second layer overlapping the bottom ends of the first.
4. Bake for 10 minutes. Turn the asparagus and bake for 5 to 15 minutes more or until tender when pierced with a knife. Serve hot or at room temperature.

Asparagus with Two Cheeses

Asparagi con Due Formaggi

Serves 4

Creamy melted cheeses and pine nuts create a rich topping for asparagus.

2 pounds thick asparagus
Salt
¼ cup freshly grated Parmigiano-Reggiano
2 ounces imported Italian fontina or Bel Paese, rind removed and thinly sliced
¼ cup chopped pine nuts
1 tablespoon fine dry bread crumbs

1. Preheat the oven to 450°F. Arrange an oven rack on the highest level. Butter a 13- × 9- × 2-inch baking dish.

2. Soak the asparagus in cold water for 10 minutes. Trim off the tough lower portion of each stalk where the color changes from green to white.

3. Pour about 1 inch of water into a large skillet and bring to a boil. Add salt to taste and the asparagus. Cook until the asparagus is partially tender, about 5 minutes. Drain well.

4. Place a layer of asparagus in the baking dish; add a second layer with the tips overlapping the bottom ends of the first layer. Sprinkle with the Parmigiano, then cover with the slices of fontina. Sprinkle with the nuts and bread crumbs.

5. Bake for 15 minutes, or until the cheese is melted and the nuts are browned. Serve hot.

Broccoli with Garlic Chips

Broccoli Aglio e Olio

Serves 4 to 6

Slowly cooked garlic slices are crisp and mellow. Do not be tempted to turn up the heat or the garlic will blacken and become bitter.

Although you need a cup of oil to cook the garlic chips, you will not need that much to dress the broccoli. Save the remaining oil in a jar in the refrigerator and use it to flavor other vegetables, pasta, or focaccia.

1 large head garlic
1 cup extra-virgin olive oil
Salt
1 large bunch broccoli
Pinch of crushed red pepper

1. Break up the garlic into individual cloves. Trim off the stem ends and peel off the skin. Cut the cloves into thin slices.

2. In a small saucepan, cook the oil and garlic over very low heat until the garlic is golden, about 15 minutes. Strain the garlic out of the oil and set both aside.

3. Bring a large pot of salted water to a boil. Meanwhile, trim the broccoli and cut it into florets. Peel the stems.

4. Add the broccoli to the boiling water and cook until tender, about 5 minutes. Drain.

5. In a bowl, toss the broccoli with about ¼ cup of the garlic oil, the pepper, and salt to taste. Sprinkle with the garlic chips. Serve at room temperature.

BROCCOLI RABE WITH PROSCIUTTO

Broccoli di Rape con Prosciutto

Serves 4

¼ cup extra-virgin olive oil
2 large garlic cloves, peeled and chopped
2 ounces sliced prosciutto, cut into thin strips
1 pound broccoli rabe, tough stems removed
Salt and freshly ground black pepper

1. In a large pot, heat the olive oil over medium heat. Add the garlic and prosciutto and stir 3 or 4 times. Add the broccoli rabe and salt and pepper to taste and stir well.

2. Cover and cook over medium-low heat, stirring occasionally, until the broccoli is tender, about 20 minutes. Add a few tablespoons of water if the broccoli starts to become dry. Serve warm or at room temperature.

CARROTS MARINATED WITH MINT AND VINEGAR

Carote a Scapece

Serves 8

Foods cooked *a scapece*, with vinegar and mint, are common throughout Italy. Some historians feel that the name is derived from that of Apicius, the person or persons who authored the earliest known cookbook, *De Re Coquinaria*.

This recipe can also be prepared with zucchini or eggplant.

2 pounds carrots
Vegetable oil for frying
3 tablespoons red wine vinegar
2 large garlic cloves, peeled and finely chopped
¼ cup chopped fresh mint or basil
Salt and freshly ground black pepper

1. Peel and trim the carrots and cut into ¼-inch-thick slices.
2. In a large heavy skillet, add oil to a depth of 1 inch. Heat the oil over medium heat until the temperature reaches 375°F on a deep-frying thermometer.
3. Dry the carrot slices with paper towels. Carefully place enough carrots to fit without crowding in the hot oil. Cook until lightly browned around the edges, about 3 minutes. With a slotted spoon, transfer the carrots to paper towels to drain. Fry the remainder in the same way.
4. When all the carrots have been cooked, transfer them to a large bowl. Sprinkle with the vinegar, garlic, mint, and salt and pepper to taste. Toss to coat.
5. Cover and refrigerate for at least 24 hours before serving. These keep well for several days.

ROASTED CAULIFLOWER

Cavolfiore al Forno

Serves 4

The dry heat of an oven does wonders for many vegetables, concentrating the flavor and bringing out their natural sweetness. Cauliflower, which can be boring, responds well to roasting, as do asparagus and green beans. A touch of olive oil helps the browning.

1 medium cauliflower
¼ cup extra-virgin olive oil
Salt

1. Preheat the oven to 350°F. Cut the cauliflower into 1- to 2-inch florets.
2. Place the cauliflower in a small roasting pan and toss with the oil and a sprinkling of salt. Bake, stirring occasionally, for 45 minutes, or until tender and lightly browned.
3. With a slotted spoon, remove the cauliflower from the pan. Serve at room temperature.

FRIED EGGPLANT

Melanzane Fritte

Serves 8

Crisp, crusty eggplant slices are delicious hot or cold. A light dusting of flour applied before the egg and bread-crumb coating keeps the eggplant from absorbing excess oil. These can be served as is or dressed with the light Tomato Sauce on page 57.

1 large eggplant (about 1½ pounds)
Salt
2 large eggs
¼ cup freshly grated Parmigiano-Reggiano
2 tablespoons water
Freshly ground black pepper
½ cup all-purpose flour
2 cups bread crumbs
Vegetable oil for frying

1. Trim the eggplant and cut crosswise into ¼-inch slices. Sprinkle lightly on both sides with salt. Stand the slices in a colander set over a plate and drain for 1 hour. Rinse off the salt with cool water and dry the slices with paper towels.

2. In a medium bowl, beat the eggs, cheese, water, and pepper to taste until well combined. Dip the eggplant into the flour, then into the egg mixture and then into the bread crumbs, patting to coat both sides. Place the slices on a wire rack to dry for 15 minutes.

3. In a large heavy skillet, heat about ½ inch of oil to 375°F. Add the eggplant slices a few at a time without crowding. Fry until golden brown, turning once, about 3 minutes on each side.

4. Drain the slices on paper towels. Keep them warm in a low oven while frying the remainder.

EGGPLANT

Melanzane

In Southern Italy, particularly Sicily, versatile eggplants are often used in place of meat. They are fried, stuffed, baked, boiled, used in salads and stews, and combined with pasta or rice. The most familiar variety is large with glossy skin like dark purple satin. At certain times of the year, round white eggplants, long, thin violet-striped Japanese eggplants, and baby or Italian varieties also appear. Whatever the variety, any eggplant should be firm and have taut, smooth skin. Don't buy eggplants that are overgrown, soft, bruised, or with brownish spots.

I prefer to leave the skin on when cooking eggplants since it helps to

SPICY EGGPLANT

Melanzane Piccanti

Serves 6

A little square off the Piazza Navona is the location of one of Rome's more unusual restaurants, called Cul de Sac. Open shelves stacked with bottles of some of Italy's finest wines reach to the ceiling over the heads of the diners. When one is requested, the waiter retrieves it with a grocer's hook. Little nets are stretched over the tables like safety nets at the circus to prevent bottles from landing on patrons.

No hot food is served, only an assortment of wonderful cheeses, cold meats, and excellent wines with thick slices of rough country bread, and a few cold, cooked vegetable dishes, including these spicy eggplant slices.

Although eggplant slices are often fried, this oven method uses less oil and is less rich. Use a jelly-roll or similar low-sided pan so that excess oil does not drip onto the oven floor.

2 medium eggplants (about 1 pound each)
Salt
Extra-virgin olive oil
2 garlic cloves, peeled and crushed
2 cups tomato puree
½ teaspoon crushed red pepper
½ cup torn fresh basil leaves

1. Trim the eggplants and cut them lengthwise into ¼-inch-thick slices. Layer the slices in a colander set over a bowl, sprinkling each layer lightly with salt. Let drain for about 1 hour.
2. Preheat the oven to 450°F. Brush two large jelly-roll pans with oil. Rinse off the salt from the eggplant slices and pat them dry. Arrange the slices in a single layer in the pans. Brush with oil. Bake for 10 minutes, turn, and bake for 10 minutes more, or until lightly browned and tender.
3. Meanwhile, in a small saucepan, cook the garlic in ¼ cup olive oil over medium heat until golden, about 2 minutes. Add the tomato puree and pepper. Simmer for 15 minutes, or until thick.

4. In a shallow dish, arrange half the eggplant slices in a single layer. Spread with half the sauce and sprinkle with half the basil. Repeat with the remaining ingredients. Serve at room temperature.

EGGPLANT WITH ANCHOVY SAUCE

Melanzane con Acciughe

Serves 4

1 large eggplant (about 1½ pounds)
Salt
Extra-virgin olive oil
1 garlic clove, peeled and finely chopped
6 anchovy fillets, chopped
1 tablespoon chopped flat-leaf parsley
2 tablespoons red wine vinegar

1. Cut the eggplant into ½-inch-thick slices. Layer the slices in a colander, sprinkling each layer lightly with salt. Place the colander over a plate and let the eggplant slices drain for about 1 hour.

2. Preheat the oven to 450°F. Rinse off the salt from the eggplant slices and pat them dry. Brush a jelly-roll pan with olive oil and arrange the eggplant slices in a single layer in it. Brush the tops with additional oil. Bake the slices for 10 minutes on each side, or until lightly browned and tender.

3. Meanwhile, in a small skillet, combine 3 tablespoons olive oil and the garlic. Cook, stirring, over medium heat until fragrant, about 1 minute. Stir in the anchovies, mashing them with the back of a spoon. Stir in the parsley and vinegar and cook for 1 minute more. Remove from the heat and set aside.

4. Arrange overlapping slices of half of the eggplant on a platter. Pour on half of the anchovy sauce. Top with the remaining eggplant and sauce. Let stand for at least 1 hour before serving. Serve at room temperature. This can be made up to 2 days ahead of serving.

retain the shape and looks attractive. The only reason to remove the skin is if the eggplant has been waxed, in which case the skin will look and feel greasy.

Most recipes call for salting eggplants to draw out the bitter juices. Be sure to rinse off the excess salt and dry the eggplants well before proceeding with the recipe.

ROASTED PEPPERS

Peperoni Arrostiti

Smoky-sweet roasted peppers are good on their own, or they may be used as an ingredient in many other recipes. All types of peppers can be prepared this way but sweet bell peppers are the kind most frequently used. Choose peppers that have smooth skins and thick, firm flesh. The red and yellow varieties are particularly sweet-tasting and beautiful when served overlapping each other. For salads, I like a combination of red, yellow, and green.

A barbecue grill does a good job of roasting peppers—especially during the warm months when you may not want to turn on the oven. If you need only one or two

EGGPLANT AND PEPPER TERRINE

Sformato di Melanzane e Peperoni

Serves 12

Layers of roasted peppers and tender eggplant are interspersed with garlic and basil in this flavorful terrine.

2 large eggplants (about 1½ pounds each)
Salt
Extra-virgin olive oil
4 large red bell peppers, roasted, seeded, and peeled (see at left)
½ cup chopped fresh basil
4 large garlic cloves, peeled and finely chopped
¼ cup red wine vinegar
Freshly ground black pepper
Fresh basil leaves

1. Trim the eggplants and cut them lengthwise into ¼-inch-thick slices. Sprinkle lightly with salt. Stand the slices in a colander set over a plate. Let drain for 1 hour.

2. Preheat the oven to 450°F. Brush two large jelly-roll pans with oil.

3. Rinse the eggplant slices in cool water and dry well. Arrange the eggplant in the pans in a single layer. Brush the tops with oil. Bake the eggplant until tender and lightly browned, turning once, about 20 minutes.

4. Meanwhile, drain the peppers and cut them into 1-inch strips. Combine the chopped basil and garlic.

5. Line an 8- × 4- × 3-inch loaf pan with plastic wrap. Place a layer of eggplant slices in the bottom of the pan, overlapping them slightly. Make a layer of roasted peppers over the eggplant. Sprinkle with some of the basil and garlic mixture, vinegar, oil, and salt and pepper to taste. Continue layering until all of the ingredients are used, packing each layer in firmly. Cover with plastic wrap and weight the terrine with a second loaf pan filled with heavy cans. Refrigerate for at least 24 hours or up to 3 days.

6. Invert the terrine onto a serving plate and remove the plastic wrap. Garnish with the basil leaves. To serve, cut into ¾-inch slices.

STEAMED ESCAROLE WITH ANCHOVIES AND OLIVES

Scarola Affogata

Serves 6

Escarole looks like coarse lettuce but it has a much more intense flavor. It can be eaten raw in salads, makes a delicious addition to soups or bean dishes, and stands up well to assertive ingredients like olives, garlic, and anchovies.

1 large bunch escarole (about 1½ pounds)
2 large garlic cloves, peeled and finely chopped
½ teaspoon crushed red pepper
¼ cup extra-virgin olive oil
6 anchovy fillets, chopped
½ cup green olives, pitted and sliced

1. Trim the escarole, removing any bruised or brown leaves and cutting off the stem end. Separate the bunch into leaves. Fill the sink or a large pan with cold water and wash the escarole well. Lift the escarole out of the water and repeat washing and draining until no trace of sand remains. Drain the escarole well. Stack the leaves and cut them crosswise into 1-inch-wide strips.

2. In a large saucepan, cook the garlic and pepper in the olive oil over medium heat for 1 minute, or until fragrant.

3. Add the escarole and cook, stirring frequently, for 5 minutes.

4. Stir in the anchovies and olives. Lower the heat. Cover and cook for 10 minutes, or until tender. Serve at room temperature.

peppers, try roasting them over an open flame on a gas stove or directly on the heating element of an electric stove. However you do them, the idea is to lightly char the skin. This causes it to blister and pull away from the flesh of the peppers and makes it easy to remove. The light charring also gives the peppers a delicious smoky flavor and aroma.

Roasted peppers should be cooked just enough to soften them slightly and make the skin easy to remove. Some recipes suggest peeling the roasted peppers under running water. This may facilitate removing the skin, but it also washes away the delicious pepper juices.

I usually make a big batch of roasted peppers at one time. At the end of the summer when red and yellow peppers are very inexpensive and plentiful, I often roast

(continued)

some to put away in the freezer. Packed in small containers, they maintain their texture and flavor well and brighten up any winter meal. Don't dress them with oil or seasonings before freezing as these ingredients do not always freeze well. Roasted peppers will keep in the refrigerator up to one week or in the freezer for up to three months.

To roast peppers preheat the broiler or grill. Wash the peppers and dry them well. Arrange them on the broiler pan or grill rack and place them 2 to 3 inches from the source of the heat. Broil or grill, turning the peppers to cook them on all sides, until they are charred in places and the skin is blistered. Be sure to turn them often so that they do not burn; use tongs and handle the peppers carefully so that the juices do not escape.

Transfer the peppers to a bowl. Cover tightly to

ESCAROLE PIE

Pizza di Scarola

Serves 8

Don't let the word *pizza* mislead you. In this case pizza means a thick, double-crust pie filled with escarole, olives, garlic, and anchovies. It is a Neapolitan classic, traditionally served on Christmas Eve.

My mother always made pizza scarola in a heavy black cast-iron skillet on top of the stove. When the bottom of the pie was browned, she would flip it and cook it slowly on the other side. That method can be tricky, so I recommend baking it instead. The result is just as tasty and a lot less oily.

Crust

2½ cups all-purpose flour

1 teaspoon salt

¼ teaspoon freshly ground black pepper

⅓ cup extra-virgin olive oil

7 to 8 tablespoons ice water

Filling

3 pounds escarole

Salt

½ cup extra-virgin olive oil

3 garlic cloves, peeled and finely chopped

1 2-ounce can anchovy fillets with their liquid

3 tablespoons chopped capers

½ cup imported black olives, such as Kalamata, pitted and sliced

1. In a large bowl, combine the flour, salt, and pepper. Drizzle with the oil, stirring with a wooden spoon until the mixture is crumbly. Add 2 tablespoons of the water and stir, adding more water as needed, until the mixture begins to hold together and form a dough. Shape into a ball. Divide the dough and shape into two disks, one twice as large as the other. Wrap each disk separately in plastic wrap and let rest for 30 minutes.

2. Trim the escarole, removing any bruised or brown leaves and cutting off the stem ends. Separate the bunches into leaves. Wash the leaves in several changes of cool water. In a large pot combine the escarole with 1 cup water and 1 teaspoon salt. Cover and cook over medium heat until tender, about 15 minutes. Drain well and let cool. Remove the excess water from the escarole by wrapping it in a cloth towel and squeezing it firmly. Coarsely chop the escarole.

3. In a large skillet, heat the olive oil over medium heat. Stir in the garlic, anchovies with their liquid, capers, and olives, mashing the anchovies with a wooden spoon. Add the escarole and stir well. Reduce the heat to low and cook, stirring occasionally, for about 10 minutes. Add salt and pepper to taste. Let cool.

4. Preheat the oven to 375°F. Lightly oil an 8- × 2-inch round cake pan.

5. On a lightly floured surface, roll out the larger piece of dough to a 15-inch circle. (Since it is made with oil, the dough will be a little stiff and resistant to stretching.) Fit the dough into the prepared pan, pressing it against the sides and letting the excess dough hang over the edge.

6. Spoon the escarole mixture into the pan. Roll out the remaining dough to a 9-inch circle and place it over the filling. Roll up the edges of the dough together, pressing against the side of the pan to seal. Cut several slits in the top of the dough with a small knife to allow steam to escape.

7. Bake for 45 minutes or until lightly browned. Let cool for 10 minutes on a wire rack. Place a plate over the pan and invert the pie onto it. Cover with a second plate and turn the pie right side up. Serve at room temperature.

keep the steam in and let cool. Cut the peppers in half and drain the juices into a bowl. Cut away the stems and cores, scraping out any remaining seeds with a spoon. Peel off and discard the skins. Place the peppers in another bowl and strain the juices over them.

FENNEL WITH PARMESAN CHEESE

Finocchio al Parmigiano

Serves 4 to 6

Fennel is usually eaten raw in salads or after a meal as a *digestivo*, but it is also good when baked to a melting tenderness and topped with Parmesan cheese.

2 small fennel bulbs (about 1 pound)
Salt
3 tablespoons extra-virgin olive oil
Freshly ground black pepper
¼ cup freshly grated Parmigiano-Reggiano

1. Preheat the oven to 450°F. Oil a 13- × 9- × 2-inch baking dish.
2. Trim off the green tops of the fennel down to the bulb. If the outer layer is bruised, remove and discard it. Slice off a thin layer from the root end. Cut the bulbs lengthwise through the core into ¼-inch-thick slices.
3. In a large pot, bring 3 quarts of water to a boil. Add the fennel and 1 teaspoon salt. Reduce the heat and simmer, uncovered, for 8 to 10 minutes or until the fennel is crisp-tender. Drain well and pat dry.
4. Arrange the fennel slices in a single layer in the prepared dish. Sprinkle with the oil and salt and pepper to taste. Top with the cheese. Bake for 10 minutes, or until the cheese is lightly browned. Serve warm or at room temperature.

MUSHROOMS IN TOMATO AND ANCHOVY SAUCE

Funghi in Salsa con Acciughe

Serves 4

Anchovies have a way of adding subtle flavor to foods without making their presence obvious. Here they enhance white mushrooms in a fresh tomato sauce. This dish would be a nice complement to an assortment of grilled vegetables.

1 large garlic clove, peeled and finely chopped
¼ cup extra-virgin olive oil
1 pound white mushrooms, halved or quartered if large
2 medium tomatoes, peeled, seeded, and chopped
5 anchovy fillets, finely chopped
1½ tablespoons chopped flat-leaf parsley
½ teaspoon salt
Freshly ground black pepper

1. In a large skillet, cook the garlic in the oil over medium heat until the garlic is fragrant, about 1 minute. Add the mushrooms and cook, stirring frequently, for 10 to 15 minutes, or until the juices evaporate and the mushrooms begin to brown. Stir in the tomatoes, anchovies, 1 tablespoon of the parsley, the salt, and pepper to taste. Bring to a simmer and cook for 5 minutes more, or until the sauce is thickened.
2. Spoon into a dish and sprinkle with the remaining parsley. Serve warm or at room temperature.

CLEANING MUSHROOMS

Though many cookbooks state that cultivated mushrooms should not be washed, I find that is really the only way to clean them thoroughly. The secret is not to let them soak in the water.

To clean cultivated mushrooms, fill a large bowl with cool water. Add the mushrooms and swirl them rapidly. Lift the mushrooms out of the water and dry them gently with a towel. If the stem ends look dry, trim them with a small knife.

Wild mushrooms such as shiitake, portobello, or porcini need only to be wiped clean with a damp paper towel.

MUSHROOMS TRUFFLE-STYLE

Funghi Trifolati

Serves 4

Mushrooms such as shiitake and portobello are really cultivated mushrooms, but they are called "wild" to distinguish them from white mushrooms. The earthy taste of shiitake or other such "wild" mushrooms makes this a memorable antipasto. Serve with crusty bread.

8 ounces shiitake mushrooms
1 tablespoon finely chopped garlic
½ cup extra-virgin olive oil
¼ cup finely chopped flat-leaf parsley
Salt and freshly ground black pepper

1. Wipe the mushroom caps with a damp cloth. Remove and discard the stems. Cut the caps into ¼-inch slices.
2. In a medium skillet, cook the garlic in the oil over medium heat until the garlic is fragrant, about 1 minute. Add the mushrooms and reduce the heat to medium low. Cook, stirring occasionally, until the mushrooms are tender, about 10 minutes.
3. Stir in the parsley and salt and pepper to taste. Serve hot.

GRILLED WILD MUSHROOMS

Funghi alla Griglia

Serves 2 to 4

Nepitella is an herb that Tuscans use to enhance the flavor of mushrooms. It grows wild along the roadsides and you often see people gathering *nepitella* to dry at home. It has a delicately minty, citruslike flavor. The English name for it is calamint, but unless you grow it yourself, it is not easy to find. I use a combination of fresh parsley and dried marjoram as a substitute, but you can use rosemary if you prefer.

Mushrooms prepared this way have a satisfying, meaty texture. The Italians even serve them as a main dish.

8 ounces large shiitake, porcini, or portobello mushrooms
3 tablespoons extra-virgin olive oil
2 large garlic cloves, peeled and finely chopped
1 tablespoon chopped flat-leaf parsley
Pinch of dried marjoram
Salt and freshly ground black pepper

1. Preheat the broiler or grill.
2. Wipe the mushrooms clean with a damp paper towel. Trim off the stems. Discard the shiitake stems; if using porcini or portobello mushrooms thinly slice the stems.
3. In a small bowl, combine the oil, garlic, parsley, marjoram, and salt and pepper to taste.
4. Brush the mushroom caps (and stems, if any) with the oil mixture. Arrange them on the grill or broiler pan with the rounded sides toward the heat. Grill for 2 minutes. Turn the caps (and stems) over and brush again with oil. Grill until tender and lightly browned, 2 to 3 minutes more. Serve hot or at room temperature.

BAKED MUSHROOMS AND GARLIC

Funghi e Aglio al Forno

Serves 4

Roasted garlic has a mild, nutty flavor and creamy texture. Serve the garlic and mushrooms with good, crusty bread.

1 head garlic
1½ pounds white mushrooms, quartered or halved if large
⅓ cup extra-virgin olive oil
2 or 3 sprigs fresh thyme or a pinch of dried
Salt and freshly ground black pepper

1. Preheat the oven to 400°F. Break up the garlic into individual cloves. Trim off the stem ends and peel off the skin.
2. In a roasting pan just large enough to hold all the ingredients in a single layer, combine the garlic, mushrooms, oil, thyme, and salt and pepper to taste.
3. Bake, stirring every 10 minutes, until the mushrooms and garlic are browned and tender, about 40 minutes. Serve warm.

SWEET AND SOUR ONIONS

Cipolline in Agrodolce

Serves 4

Warm baby onions in a sweet and sour glaze are a delicious antipasto. They can be prepared ahead of time and reheated just before serving but they should not be served cold since the butter will solidify.

2 pounds very small white onions
4 tablespoons unsalted butter
2 cups homemade beef broth or 1 13¾-ounce can beef broth combined with enough water to equal 2 cups
¼ cup white wine vinegar
1½ tablespoons sugar
Salt and freshly ground black pepper

1. Bring a large pot of water to a boil. Add the onions and cook for 30 seconds. Drain and cool under cold running water.
2. With a sharp paring knife, shave off the tip of the root ends; do not slice off the ends too deeply or the onions will fall apart during cooking. Remove the skins.
3. In a large heavy skillet over medium heat, combine the onions, butter, and beef broth. Cover and cook, stirring occasionally, for 30 minutes.
4. Uncover and stir in the vinegar, sugar, and salt and pepper to taste. Reduce the heat to low and cook, uncovered, shaking the pan occasionally, until the onions are very tender when pierced with a fork, about 30 minutes. Add a little warm water if needed to keep the onions moist. Serve warm.

LITTLE SHALLOTS IN VERMOUTH

Piccoli Scalogni in Vermut

Serves 6 to 8

Sometimes I can find tiny shallots at the market. They would be a nuisance to use in recipes where they need to be chopped but they are perfect for roasting or braising.

Either sweet red or dry white vermouth can be used here. In addition to being a delicious antipasto, these shallots are good as an accompaniment to roasted chicken, veal, or pork. Small onions may also be prepared this way.

1 pound small shallots
3 tablespoons extra-virgin olive oil
½ cup red or white vermouth
Salt and freshly ground black pepper

1. Bring a large pot of water to a boil. Add the shallots, bring back to a boil, and cook 5 minutes. Drain the shallots and run them under cold water until cool enough to handle.

2. With a sharp paring knife, trim off the root end of each shallot and slip off the skins. If necessary, trim skin from the tops. Divide any doubled bulbs.

3. In a skillet large enough to hold the shallots in a single layer, heat the oil over medium-high heat. Add the shallots and cook, stirring frequently, until they are lightly browned. Add the vermouth and salt and pepper to taste.

4. Reduce the heat to medium low, cover, and cook until tender, stirring occasionally, about 10 minutes. Serve warm or at room temperature.

SAUTÉED PEPPERS WITH TOMATO, ONIONS, AND OLIVES

Peperonata

Serves 4 to 6

Many versions of peperonata are made throughout Italy, but I especially like this one, which has big green Sicilian olives. Serve peperonata on toasted bread, as the filling for a frittata, or as a side dish with grilled meat. Once, at Ristorante Vipore in the hills outside of Lucca, we were served peperonata made without olives as a sauce for a succulent roast loin of pork.

¼ **cup extra-virgin olive oil**
**2 large red bell peppers, cored, seeded, and
  sliced**
**2 large green bell peppers, cored, seeded, and
  sliced**
2 large onions, peeled and sliced
1 large tomato, peeled, seeded, and chopped
¼ **cup sliced pitted green olives, preferably
  Sicilian**
2 tablespoons red wine vinegar
Salt

1. In a large skillet, heat the oil over medium heat. Add the peppers and cook, stirring frequently, for 10 minutes.
2. Add the onions and cook until the vegetables are tender and lightly browned, about 10 minutes more.
3. Stir in the tomato, olives, vinegar, and salt to taste. Cover and cook until the liquid has evaporated, about 10 minutes more. Serve at room temperature.

POTATO CROQUETTES

Panzerotti

Makes 2 dozen croquettes

In my family, these crusty pillows of mashed potatoes and cheese, one of my mother's specialties, were an important part of every holiday meal. Panzerotti can be served as an antipasto or as a *contorno* (side dish) with roasted meats.

2 pounds boiling potatoes (about 5 large), peeled
Salt
3 large eggs, separated
½ cup freshly grated Parmigiano-Reggiano
Freshly ground black pepper
2 ounces mozzarella, cut into ¼-inch cubes
   (about ⅓ cup)
1½ cups fine dry bread crumbs
Vegetable oil for frying

1. Place the potatoes in a medium saucepan with cold water to cover. Add salt to taste, cover, and bring to a boil. Cook over medium heat until the potatoes are tender when pierced with a fork. Drain the potatoes and mash them with a masher or by pressing them through a food mill or ricer. Let cool slightly.
2. Stir in the egg yolks and Parmigiano. Add salt and pepper to taste.
3. Using about 3 tablespoons of the mixture, shape it into a 2½- × 1-inch log; repeat with the remaining potatoes. Poke a few pieces of mozzarella into each log, smoothing the potato mixture around them to completely enclose the cheese.
4. In a shallow dish, beat the egg whites until frothy. Spread the bread crumbs on a sheet of wax paper. Dip the potato logs into the egg whites, then roll them in the bread crumbs, and pat them so that the crumbs adhere. Place on a wire rack and let dry for 15 to 30 minutes.

5. Pour about ½ inch of oil into a deep heavy frying pan. Heat over medium heat. Fry the panzerotti a few at a time until golden brown, turning them once. Drain on paper towels. Serve immediately, or set aside at room temperature until serving time and reheat in a 350°F oven for 10 to 15 minutes.

SAUTÉED PEPPERS WITH BALSAMIC VINEGAR

Peperoni in Aceto Balsamico

Serves 6 to 8

The sweet-tart flavor of balsamic vinegar adds a subtle richness to bright red and yellow peppers. The peppers need long, slow cooking to tenderize them and bring out all their flavor.

¼ cup extra-virgin olive oil
3 large red bell peppers, cored, seeded, and thinly sliced
3 large yellow bell peppers, cored, seeded, and thinly sliced
1 teaspoon sugar
½ teaspoon salt
3 tablespoons balsamic vinegar

1. In a large heavy skillet, heat the oil over medium-low heat. Add the peppers and cook, stirring occasionally, until tender and spotted with brown, about 25 minutes. (Do not raise the heat to speed up the cooking or the peppers will burn.)
2. Add the sugar, salt, and vinegar and stir well. Simmer until most of the liquid has evaporated, about 5 minutes more. Serve warm.

ROASTED RADICCHIO WITH MOZZARELLA

Radicchio al Forno con la Mozzarella

Serves 4 to 6

Creamy smooth melted mozzarella tops wedges of slightly bitter radicchio, for a nice contrast of both color and flavor.

2 medium heads radicchio (about 8 ounces each)
¼ cup extra-virgin olive oil
Salt and freshly ground black pepper
8 ounces fresh mozzarella, cut into 16 slices

1. Preheat the oven to 400°F. Lightly oil an 11- × 8- × 2-inch baking dish.
2. Rinse the radicchio and remove any discolored or bruised leaves. Trim a thin slice off the stem ends. Cut each head into 8 wedges.
3. In a small bowl, combine the olive oil and salt and pepper to taste. Place the wedges cut side down in the prepared baking pan and brush with the seasoned oil. Bake for 10 to 15 minutes or until the radicchio is tender and browned.
4. Top each wedge of radicchio with a slice of mozzarella. Bake just until the mozzarella begins to melt, about 2 minutes more. Serve immediately.

BRAISED RADICCHIO WITH PANCETTA

Radicchio Brasato con la Pancetta

Serves 8

Cooked radicchio loses its distinctive burgundy and white markings and turns a dark, tawny red. Although the color is no longer as vibrant, the flavor of cooked radicchio is richer. Try it grilled, in risotto, or braised as in this recipe, inspired by one from a favorite New York restaurant, Dal Barone.

2 medium heads radicchio (about 8 ounces each)
2 tablespoons extra-virgin olive oil
2 ounces thickly sliced pancetta, cut into ¼-inch dice
¼ cup finely chopped onion
Salt and freshly ground black pepper
3 tablespoons red wine vinegar
¼ cup water
1½ teaspoons sugar

1. Rinse the radicchio and remove any discolored or bruised leaves. Trim a thin slice off the stem ends. Cut each head into 8 wedges; be sure to cut through the core so that the wedges hold together when cooked.
2. In a large skillet, heat the olive oil over medium heat. Add the pancetta and cook until the edges are golden, about 5 minutes. Add the onion and cook until tender, about 5 minutes more.
3. Arrange the wedges of radicchio in the skillet in a single layer. Sprinkle with salt and pepper to taste. In a small bowl, combine the vinegar, water, and sugar and pour over the radicchio.
4. Cover the skillet and cook, turning the radicchio once, until tender, about 12 minutes. Serve warm or at room temperature.

SPINACH

Fresh spinach has an incomparable flavor but like most leafy vegetables, it requires a lot of cleaning to eliminate any sand. To do so, fill the sink or a large basin with cool water. Add the spinach and swish it around. Let stand for several minutes to allow the sand to drop to the bottom. Lift the spinach out of the water, drain the water, and rinse away the sand. Repeat the whole operation several more times until there is no sand left in the bottom of the sink.

Frozen spinach is not as flavorful as the fresh vegetable, but it can be substituted in recipes where further cooking is required. For best results, cook frozen spinach for only 2 or 3 minutes or just until thawed.

SPINACH AND RICOTTA TART

Torta di Ricotta e Spinaci

Serves 6 to 8

Whenever I make my favorite ravioli, I can't resist nibbling at the delicious spinach, ricotta, and prosciutto filling. I tasted this tart when I was in Parma and knew that some clever cook had figured out another way to use that delicious stuffing. An interesting touch here is the ricotta in the pastry crust.

Crust

8 tablespoons (1 stick) unsalted butter, at room temperature
½ cup whole-milk ricotta
1½ cups all-purpose flour
½ teaspoon salt

Filling

1 pound fresh spinach or 1 10-ounce package frozen chopped spinach, thawed
4 tablespoons unsalted butter
2 tablespoons finely chopped onion
¼ cup finely chopped prosciutto (about 1 ounce)
1 large egg
½ cup plus 2 tablespoons freshly grated Parmigiano-Reggiano
½ cup heavy cream
¼ teaspoon nutmeg
1½ cups whole-milk ricotta

1. In a large bowl, beat the butter and ricotta until smooth. Stir in the flour and salt just until blended. Flatten into a disk approximately 6 inches around and wrap in plastic wrap. Chill for 1 hour or overnight.

2. On a lightly floured surface, roll out the dough to an 11-inch circle. Drape the dough over the rolling pin and transfer it to a 9-inch tart pan with a removable bottom. Press the dough into the bottom of the pan and up the sides without stretching it. Trim off all but a ½-inch overhang. Fold in the overhang and press it against the side of the pan. Cover and refrigerate for at least 30 minutes.

3. If using fresh spinach, wash the spinach in a large pan of cool water, changing the water several times until there are no traces of sand left at the bottom of the pan. Remove the tough stems. Place the spinach in a large pot, cover, and cook over medium heat until the spinach is tender, about 5 minutes. Drain and let cool. Wrap the spinach in a cotton towel and squeeze to extract as much liquid as possible. Finely chop the spinach.

4. In a small skillet, melt the butter over medium heat. Add the onion and cook until tender, about 5 minutes. Add the prosciutto and cook for 1 minute. Stir in the spinach and cook for 2 minutes more.

5. Preheat the oven to 450°F. Butter a 12-inch piece of aluminum foil. Line the pastry shell with the foil, buttered side down. Fill the shell with pie weights or dried beans and bake for 10 minutes. Remove the weights and foil and prick the bottom of the shell all over with a fork. Bake for another 5 minutes, or until the pastry is just set and the edges are lightly golden. Remove the shell from the oven. Reduce the oven temperature to 375°F.

6. In a bowl, beat together the egg, the ½ cup Parmigiano, the cream, and nutmeg. Stir in the spinach and ricotta. Scrape the mixture into the shell. Sprinkle with the remaining Parmigiano. Bake for 35 minutes, or until the filling is set and the cheese is lightly golden. Serve warm.

Sweet and Sour Winter Squash

Zucca Rossa all' Agrodolce

Serves 6 to 8

The Sicilians call this unusual dish *Fegato dei Sette Cannoli*, Liver of the Seven Cannons. Seven Cannons is a district in Palermo, where the people were so poor they could not afford to buy liver or meat of any kind. Being resourceful, they cooked inexpensive squash to make it resemble a meat dish.

Any kind of winter squash can be used. The flavor improves as it marinates, so make this up to three days before serving. The squash can be fried instead of baked, but it is less oily when baked. Zucchini and eggplant can also be served this way.

Extra-virgin olive oil

1 butternut squash, small pumpkin, or other winter squash (about 2 pounds)

⅓ cup red wine vinegar

1 tablespoon sugar

½ teaspoon salt

2 garlic cloves, peeled and finely chopped

⅓ cup chopped fresh mint, basil, or flat-leaf parsley

1. Preheat the oven to 400°F. Generously brush two jelly-roll pans with olive oil.

2. Cut the squash in half lengthwise. Scrape out the seeds and membranes. Peel the squash and cut it into ¼-inch-thick slices.

3. Arrange the squash in the pans in a single layer. Brush the slices with additional oil. Bake for 20 minutes. Turn the slices and bake for 15 to 20 minutes, or until tender and lightly browned.

4. In a small saucepan, heat the vinegar, sugar, and salt and stir until the sugar and salt are dissolved.

5. Arrange a single layer of the squash in a shallow dish. Sprinkle with some of the garlic and mint. Continue layering the remaining squash, sprinkling each layer with herbs. Pour the vinegar mixture over all. Cover and refrigerate for at least 24 hours before serving.

TOMATOES WITH GRAPES

Pomodori con Uva

Serves 4

Da Delfina in Artimino, near Florence, specializes in the rustic country foods of the Carmignano region. Delfina herself presides over the kitchen while her son Carlo orchestrates the dining room. One day Carlo suggested we taste a traditional peasant dish of the area, now almost forgotten. The baked tomatoes with grapes we were served were unusual, very good, and well worth reviving.

2 medium ripe tomatoes
2 cups seedless green grapes, stemmed
1 tablespoon tomato paste blended with 2
tablespoons water
2 tablespoons dry bread crumbs
½ teaspoon salt
Freshly ground black pepper
1 tablespoon extra-virgin olive oil

1. Preheat the oven to 400°F. Oil a 9-inch square baking pan.
2. Cut the tomatoes in half crosswise. Arrange them cut sides up in the pan. Scatter the grapes around the tomatoes. Pour the tomato paste over all.
3. Combine the bread crumbs, salt, pepper to taste, and the olive oil. Spoon the mixture over the tomatoes. Bake for 1 hour or until the tomatoes and grapes are very tender. Serve warm or at room temperature.

SAUTÉED ZUCCHINI WITH PEPPERS

Zucchini in Padella con Peperoni

Serves 6

Small cigar-size zucchini are the most tender and fla-vorful. Salting them draws out the excess juices so that the zucchini will brown, not steam, as they cook. In this colorful and delicious combination, roasted peppers are mixed with the zucchini. Be sure to taste the vegetables after they have chilled and adjust the seasoning as necessary.

8 small zucchini (about 1½ pounds)
Salt
½ cup extra-virgin olive oil
4 large red and/or yellow bell peppers, roasted, seeded, and peeled (see page 30–33)
2 tablespoons balsamic vinegar
¼ cup chopped fresh basil or flat-leaf parsley
1 large garlic clove, peeled and finely chopped
Freshly ground black pepper

1. With a vegetable brush, scrub the zucchini well under cold running water. Trim the ends and cut the zucchini into ½-inch cubes. Place the zucchini in a colander set over a plate and sprinkle with salt. Let drain for 1 hour. Rinse the zucchini well and dry them with paper towels.

2. In a large skillet, heat the oil over medium-high heat. Add the zucchini and cook, stirring frequently, until browned, about 10 minutes.

3. Meanwhile, drain the peppers and cut them into thin strips. Stir the peppers into the zucchini. Cook for 1 minute more.

4. Tip the skillet to draw the oil away from the vegetables. With a slotted spoon, transfer the vegetables to a bowl, draining them well to allow any excess oil to drip back into the pan. Stir in the vinegar, basil, garlic, and salt and pepper to taste. Chill slightly before serving.

STUFFED
VEGETABLES

Verdure Ripiene

I find stuffed vegetables very appealing. I like the idea of a savory stuffing wrapped in a neat individual-size package. They make particularly good antipasti and many of them, such as Sausage-Stuffed Tomatoes and Pasta-Stuffed Peppers, are substantial enough to be a main course. These stuffings, by the way, are often interchangeable. Try the pasta in the tomatoes and the sausage in the peppers.

Mangia ogni

qualita di carne,

ma evita ogni specie

di funghi.

Eat every type of

meat, but avoid

every kind of

mushroom.

*With a large knife,
trim off the top 1 inch of
the artichokes. Rinse the
artichokes under cold
water. Cut off the stem of
each artichoke to make it
even with the base so it
will stand upright. Peel
off the tough outer skin
of the stems and cook
with the artichokes.
Bend back and snap off
the small leaves around
the base. With scissors
trim the pointed tops off
the remaining leaves. As
each artichoke is fin-
ished, drop it into a large
bowl of cold water into
which you have squeezed
the juice of 1 lemon. Re-
moving the choke is op-
tional. Use a small knife
with a rounded tip to
scrape out the fuzzy
leaves in the center. Proceed with the recipe.*

STUFFED ARTICHOKES

Carciofi Ripieni

Serves 8

While enormous, dinner-plate size artichokes may look appealing, they really are not very good. Somehow they never seem to cook through, or by the time the centers are tender the leaves are overcooked. Instead, choose medium-size artichokes that look fresh and have fleshy, crisp leaves. They should feel heavy for their size and squeak like a pair of new shoes when they are lightly squeezed. Purple or brown markings on the base of the leaves indicate an artichoke that has been touched by frost, which supposedly enhances flavor and sweetness.

8 medium artichokes
1 cup dry bread crumbs
**1 cup freshly grated Parmigiano-Reggiano or
  Pecorino Romano**
⅓ cup chopped flat-leaf parsley
1 garlic clove, peeled and finely chopped
Salt and freshly ground black pepper
About 5 tablespoons extra-virgin olive oil

1. Prepare the artichokes as directed at left.
2. In a bowl, combine the bread crumbs, cheese, parsley, garlic, and salt and pepper to taste. Add 3 tablespoons olive oil or just enough to moisten the crumb mixture. Gently spread the artichoke leaves apart. Holding an artichoke in one hand over the bowl, use your other hand to stuff it with the bread-crumb mixture. Do not pack it tightly.
3. Place the artichokes in a pot just wide enough to hold them upright. Add water to a depth of ¾ inch around the artichokes.
4. Drizzle the artichokes with 2 tablespoons of the remaining oil. Cover the pot and place over medium heat. When the water comes to a simmer, reduce the heat to low. Cook until the artichoke bottoms are tender when pierced with a knife and a leaf pulls out easily, about 45 minutes; add additional water if needed to prevent scorching. Serve warm or at room temperature.

PANCETTA-STUFFED ARTICHOKES

Carciofi Ripieni con Pancetta

Serves 8

Pancetta is unsmoked Italian bacon. It looks like regular bacon except that it is rolled up instead of flat. Some manufacturers sprinkle it with a layer of coarsely ground pepper before rolling it up. If you cannot find pancetta, use prosciutto in this recipe.

8 medium artichokes
4 ounces thickly sliced pancetta
¼ cup flat-leaf parsley
2 large garlic cloves, peeled
Salt and freshly ground black pepper
¼ cup extra-virgin olive oil

1. Prepare the artichokes as directed on page 52. Peel the artichoke stems.
2. Finely chop the artichoke stems, pancetta, parsley, and garlic. Combine in a small bowl and add salt and pepper to taste.
3. Gently spread open the artichoke leaves and push the stuffing among the leaves.
4. Stand the artichokes in a pot just large enough to hold them closely together. Pour about ¾ inch of water around the artichokes. Drizzle the artichokes with the olive oil.
5. Cover the pot and bring to a simmer over medium heat; reduce the heat to low. Cook until the artichoke bottoms are tender when pierced with a knife, about 45 minutes; add water if needed to prevent scorching. Let cool to room temperature and serve.

ROASTED STUFFED ARTICHOKES WITH PINE NUTS AND RAISINS

Carciofi Ripieni al Pignoli e Uvette

Serves 4

4 medium artichokes
½ cup dry bread crumbs
4 anchovy fillets, finely chopped
2 tablespoons chopped drained capers
2 tablespoons toasted pine nuts
2 tablespoons golden raisins
2 tablespoons chopped flat-leaf parsley
1 large garlic clove, peeled and finely chopped
Salt and freshly ground pepper
½ cup extra-virgin olive oil
½ cup dry white wine

1. Prepare the artichokes as directed on page 52.

2. Preheat the oven to 400°F.

3. In a bowl, combine the bread crumbs, anchovies, capers, pine nuts, raisins, parsley, garlic, and salt and pepper to taste. Stir in ¼ cup of the olive oil.

4. Gently spread open the artichoke leaves. Stuff the artichokes loosely with the bread-crumb mixture. Stand the artichokes in a small baking dish just large enough to hold them tightly together. Pour the wine around the artichokes. Drizzle the remaining ¼ cup oil over and around the artichokes. Cover with foil. Bake for 1 hour.

5. Uncover the artichokes and bake for 5 to 10 minutes longer or until the hearts are tender when pierced in the center with a knife. If the pan becomes dry during the cooking, add a few tablespoons water. Let cool and serve at room temperature.

ARTICHOKES STUFFED WITH RICE

Carciofi Ripieni di Riso

Serves 8

Here the artichokes are cut in half lengthwise so they resemble little scoops, then stuffed with savory rice.

4 medium artichokes
Salt
¼ cup finely chopped onion
¼ cup extra-virgin olive oil
5 anchovy fillets
½ cup Arborio or other short-grain rice
¼ cup freshly grated Parmigiano-Reggiano
2 tablespoons chopped flat-leaf parsley
¼ cup dry white wine

1. Prepare the artichokes as directed on page 52.

2. Preheat the oven to 375°F. Oil a large baking pan.

3. Bring a large pot of water to a boil. Add the artichokes and salt to taste. Cook, uncovered, until the artichoke hearts are tender when pierced with a knife, about 20 minutes. Drain well. Cut the artichokes in half lengthwise. With a small knife, scoop out the fuzzy choke from the center of each artichoke half. Place the artichokes cut side up in the prepared pan.

4. Meanwhile, in a small saucepan, cook the onion in 1 tablespoon of the olive oil over medium heat until tender, about 5 minutes.

5. Stir in the anchovy fillets and mash them to a paste with a wooden spoon. Stir in the rice. Add 1 cup water and ½ teaspoon salt. Cover and cook over low heat until the rice is tender and all the liquid is absorbed, about 20 minutes.

6. Remove the rice from the heat. Stir in 3 tablespoons of the cheese and the parsley. Spoon the rice mixture into the artichoke halves. Sprinkle with the remaining cheese and olive oil. Pour the wine and ¼ cup water around the artichokes. Bake for 15 minutes or until the cheese is lightly golden. Serve warm or at room temperature.

EGGPLANT STUFFED WITH BEEF

Melanzane Ripiene

Serves 8

4 baby or Japanese eggplants (about 1½ pounds)
Salt
8 ounces lean ground beef
2 ounces sliced Genoa salami, finely chopped
  (about ½ cup)
1 large egg, lightly beaten
1 garlic clove, peeled and finely chopped
¼ cup dry bread crumbs
¼ cup grated provolone
2 tablespoons chopped flat-leaf parsley
Freshly ground black pepper
1 recipe Tomato Sauce (see page 57)

1. Preheat the oven to 375°F. Lightly oil an 11- × 8- × 2-inch baking dish.

2. Trim the stem ends from the eggplants and cut them in half lengthwise. Bring a large saucepan of water to a boil. Add the eggplants and salt to taste. Simmer for 4 minutes. Drain the eggplants and let cool.

3. With a spoon, scoop out the center of each eggplant, leaving only a ¼-inch shell. Chop the pulp and place it in a bowl. Blot the shells dry with paper towels and place them cut sides up in the prepared baking dish.

4. Add the beef, salami, egg, garlic, bread crumbs, provolone, parsley, and salt and pepper to taste to the eggplant pulp. Mix well. Spoon the mixture into the eggplant shells, rounding the tops. Spoon the Tomato Sauce over the eggplants.

5. Bake until the filling is cooked through, about 20 minutes. Serve warm or at room temperature.

TOMATO SAUCE

Sugo di Pomodoro

Makes about 2½ cups

This simple sauce is very quick to make and very versatile. It can be served on vegetables, pasta, pizza, or frittatas and can be varied in many ways. Try it with fresh parsley or dried oregano instead of the basil, or a medium onion in place of, or in addition to, the garlic.

The texture of this sauce is somewhat chunky. For a smooth sauce, pass the tomatoes through a food mill before adding them to the pot.

If using canned tomatoes, be sure to use good-quality tomatoes imported from Italy. Read the labels carefully, and don't be deceived by brands that have Italian-sounding names but come from other places. Too often, these non-Italian tomatoes are underripe when picked and packed. They don't thicken when cooked, and your sauce will be thin and sour.

¼ cup extra-virgin olive oil
1 large garlic clove, peeled and finely chopped
1 28-ounce can Italian peeled tomatoes with their
  juice, or 2 pounds ripe fresh plum tomatoes,
  peeled, seeded, and chopped
Salt and freshly ground black pepper
2 tablespoons chopped fresh basil

1. In a medium saucepan, cook the oil and garlic over medium heat until the garlic is fragrant, about 1 minute. Immediately add the tomatoes and salt and pepper to taste. Stir the tomatoes and crush them with the back of a wooden spoon.
2. Reduce the heat and simmer, stirring occasionally, until the sauce is thickened and the oil separates from the tomatoes, about 20 minutes. Just before serving, stir in the basil.

This keeps well in the refrigerator for up to 1 week or in the freezer for up to 1 month.

EGGPLANT SANDWICHES

Fette di Melanzane Ripiene

Makes about 20 sandwiches

As a variation, these "sandwiches" can be stuffed with thin slices of fontina cheese, prosciutto, and a sprinkling of basil.

2 medium eggplants (about 1 pound each)
Salt
Extra-virgin olive oil
1 2-ounce can anchovy fillets, drained and chopped
¼ cup chopped flat-leaf parsley or basil
2 tablespoons capers, drained and chopped
8 ounces fresh mozzarella, thinly sliced

1. Cut the eggplants into ¼-inch-thick slices. Layer the slices in a colander, sprinkling each layer lightly with salt. Place the colander over a plate and let drain for about 1 hour.

2. Preheat the oven to 450°F. Lightly brush two jelly-roll pans with olive oil.

3. Rinse off the salt from the eggplant and pat the slices dry. Arrange the slices in a single layer in the pans. Bake for 20 minutes, turning once, until tender and lightly browned.

4. Meanwhile, combine the anchovies, parsley, and capers.

5. Sprinkle the anchovy mixture over half of the browned eggplant slices. Top with a slice of mozzarella and another slice of eggplant. Brush with more oil. Bake for 5 minutes or until the cheese is slightly melted. Serve hot.

SPINACH-STUFFED MUSHROOMS

Funghi Ripieni di Spinaci

Serves 8

Mushrooms are a perfect vehicle for all kinds of stuffings. Here, spinach, cream, and prosciutto make a rich and delicious filling.

8 ounces spinach, washed and trimmed
12 large white mushrooms (about 14 ounces), trimmed
3 tablespoons unsalted butter
2 tablespoons finely chopped shallots or onion
¼ cup finely chopped prosciutto (about 1 ounce)
⅓ cup heavy cream
¼ cup freshly grated Parmigiano-Reggiano
Pinch of nutmeg
Salt and freshly ground black pepper

1. Preheat the oven to 400°F. Butter a 13- × 9- × 2-inch baking dish.

2. Place the spinach in a medium saucepan and cook, covered, over medium heat until wilted, about 5 minutes. Drain well and let cool.

3. Wrap the spinach in a cloth towel and squeeze to extract as much liquid as possible. Finely chop the spinach. Snap off the mushroom stems and finely chop.

4. In a medium skillet, heat 2 tablespoons of the butter over medium heat. Add the shallots and mushroom stems and cook, stirring frequently, until tender, about 5 minutes. Stir in the spinach and prosciutto. Add the cream and bring to a boil. Remove from the heat and stir in the cheese, nutmeg, and salt and pepper to taste.

5. Arrange the mushroom caps rounded sides down in the prepared dish. Spoon the spinach mixture into the mushroom caps. Melt the remaining 1 tablespoon butter and brush it over the mushrooms. Bake for 30 minutes or until tender. Serve warm.

VEAL-STUFFED MUSHROOMS

Funghi Ripieni di Vitello

Serves 8

24 medium white mushrooms
3 tablespoons unsalted butter
1 small onion, peeled and finely chopped
8 ounces ground veal
1 egg
½ cup dry bread crumbs
¼ cup freshly grated Parmigiano-Reggiano
2 tablespoons chopped flat-leaf parsley
½ teaspoon salt
Freshly ground black pepper

1. Preheat the oven to 400°F. Oil a large baking pan.

2. Snap off the mushroom stems and chop them fine.

3. In a medium skillet, heat the butter over medium heat. Add the onion and cook, stirring, until tender, about 5 minutes. Add the chopped mushroom stems and cook until tender and lightly browned, about 10 minutes.

4. In a bowl, combine the veal, egg, bread crumbs, Parmigiano, parsley, salt, and pepper to taste. Add the onion mixture and blend well. Fill the mushroom caps with this mixture, mounding the stuffing slightly.

5. Place the mushrooms in the prepared pan. Bake for 30 minutes or until the mushrooms are tender and the stuffing is browned. Serve warm.

STUFFED PEPPER WEDGES

Spicchi di Peperoni Ripieni

Serves 4 to 6

Wedges of peppers lightly stuffed with tomato, olives, and anchovies.

3 large red bell peppers
1 large ripe tomato, peeled, seeded, and chopped
1 large garlic clove, peeled and finely chopped
12 imported black olives, such as Kalamata, pitted and thinly sliced
1 2-ounce can anchovy fillets, drained and chopped
2 tablespoons chopped flat-leaf parsley
Freshly ground black pepper
¼ cup extra-virgin olive oil

1. Preheat the oven to 350°F. Oil a 13- × 9- × 2-inch baking dish.

2. Cut the peppers lengthwise into quarters and remove the seeds and white membranes. Arrange the quarters skin side down in the prepared dish.

3. In a bowl, combine the tomato, garlic, olives, anchovies, parsley, and pepper to taste. Spoon the mixture into the pepper wedges. Drizzle with the olive oil. Bake for 45 minutes or until the peppers are tender when pierced with a fork. Serve warm or cold.

PASTA-STUFFED PEPPERS

Peperoni Imbottiti

Serves 6

Short pasta sauced with tomatoes and anchovies fills these hearty baked peppers.

1 large garlic clove, peeled and finely chopped
2 tablespoons extra-virgin olive oil
3 large ripe tomatoes, peeled, seeded, and chopped
½ teaspoon dried oregano
1 2-ounce can anchovy fillets, drained and chopped
2 tablespoons drained capers
¼ cup sliced pitted Kalamata or other imported black olives
Salt and freshly ground black pepper
4 ounces ditalini, tubetti, or small pasta
6 large red, yellow, or green bell peppers

1. In a medium skillet, cook the garlic in the oil over medium heat until it is fragrant, about 1 minute. Stir in the tomatoes and oregano and cook, stirring occasionally, until most of the liquid has evaporated. Remove from the heat and stir in the anchovies, capers, olives, and salt and pepper to taste.

2. Meanwhile, bring a large pot of salted water to a boil. Add the pasta and cook until almost tender, about 5 minutes. Drain well. Combine the pasta and the tomato mixture.

3. Preheat the oven to 375°F. Oil a baking dish just large enough to hold the peppers standing upright.

4. Cut the tops off the peppers and set them aside. Remove and discard the seeds, and cut away the white membranes with a small knife. Fill the peppers about three quarters full with the pasta mixture. Place the tops on the peppers and arrange them in the prepared dish. Pour 1 cup of water around the peppers.

5. Bake for 45 minutes or until the peppers are tender when pierced with a fork. Serve warm.

STUFFED FRYING PEPPERS

Friadielli Ripieni

Serves 8

This recipe uses the long, thin, light green to red frying peppers that were called *friadielli* by my mother and aunts. We always ate these peppers as an accompaniment to grilled meats.

Choose the straightest peppers you can find as they will be easier to stuff and do not overfill them or the stuffing will spill out. Dry the peppers well to minimize spattering and use tongs to turn them gently without piercing the skin.

8 Italian frying peppers
1¼ cups dry bread crumbs
⅓ cup freshly grated Pecorino Romano or
** Parmigiano-Reggiano**
¼ cup chopped flat-leaf parsley
1 garlic clove, peeled and finely chopped
Salt and freshly ground black pepper
About ½ cup extra-virgin olive oil
1 28-ounce can crushed tomatoes
2 tablespoons finely chopped fresh basil

1. Cut off the tops of the peppers and scoop out the seeds.
2. In a bowl, combine the bread crumbs, cheese, parsley, garlic, and salt and pepper to taste. Stir in 3 tablespoons olive oil or enough to moisten the crumbs. Spoon the stuffing loosely into the peppers, leaving about 1 inch clearance at the top.
3. In a large skillet, heat ¼ cup olive oil over medium heat. Add the peppers and cook until browned on all sides, about 20 minutes.
4. Add the tomatoes, basil, and salt and pepper to taste. Bring to a simmer. Cover and cook, turning the peppers occasionally, until tender, about 15 minutes. Uncover and cook for 5 minutes more or until the sauce is thick. Serve warm or at room temperature.

ROASTED PEPPER ROLLS

Braciole di Peperoni

Serves 4 to 6

Apulia, the heel of the Italian boot, is a beautiful region with a long sunny coast and fine beaches. While passing through the city of Taranto, we decided to visit a wine maker there. Though we had not been expected, he welcomed us enthusiastically. Closing his account books, he announced to his staff that in honor of our visit, he was taking a holiday.

Not only did he show us around his winery, but to our amazement he quickly organized a tour of the region, stopping often to introduce us to family, friends, and even the local high school English teacher, of whom he was very proud. Apologizing that his wife was out of town, he took us to a tiny trattoria for lunch. The *cucina*, he said, was not as good as his wife could prepare, but it was acceptable. We thought it was great and devoured every morsel of the delectable vegetables and seafood that were served, including the tasty little rolls of stuffed roasted peppers.

The last stop on our tour was a locally renowned *pasticceria* and *gelateria*, pastry and ice cream shop, owned by a cousin of the wine maker. The shop featured the smoothest, creamiest ice creams. After a tasting, we were finally on our way once more, bearing a large tray of assorted cookies as a farewell gift and promising to return again soon to taste our new friend's wife's cooking. I can't wait.

¼ **cup dry bread crumbs**
1 **tablespoon finely chopped capers**
2 **anchovy fillets, finely chopped**
1 **tablespoon toasted pine nuts**
1 **tablespoon golden raisins**
1 **tablespoon grated Pecorino Romano**
Freshly ground black pepper

2 tablespoons extra-virgin olive oil
4 large red and/or yellow bell peppers, roasted,
seeded, and peeled (see pages 30–33)
1 tablespoon chopped flat-leaf parsley

1. Preheat the oven to 375°F. Oil an 8-inch square baking dish.

2. In a bowl, combine the bread crumbs, capers, anchovies, pine nuts, raisins, cheese, pepper to taste, and 1 tablespoon of the olive oil.

3. Drain the peppers. Sprinkle a spoonful of the bread-crumb mixture over the inside of each pepper half. Roll up the peppers and place them in the prepared dish. Sprinkle with the parsley and the remaining 1 tablespoon oil.

4. Bake for 20 minutes, or until the peppers are heated through. Serve warm or at room temperature.

PEPPERS WITH FONTINA AND PROSCIUTTO

Peperoni con Fontina e Prosciutto

Serves 4

2 large red bell peppers, roasted, seeded, and
peeled (see pages 30–33)
4 thin slices prosciutto
4 thin slices Italian fontina or Bel Paese
Extra-virgin olive oil
1 tablespoon chopped flat-leaf parsley

1. Preheat the oven to 400°F. Oil a small baking dish.

2. Drain the peppers. Fold a slice of prosciutto and place it with a fontina slice inside each pepper half.

3. Arrange the peppers in the baking dish and brush them with olive oil.

4. Bake for 10 minutes, or until the cheese has melted. Sprinkle with the parsley. Serve warm.

GRANDMOTHER'S STUFFED PEPPERS

Peperoni Imbottiti alla Nonna

Serves 4

Procida, a tiny island off the coast of Naples, was the birthplace of my father's mother, who came to America around the turn of the century. Grandma was a wonderful cook and many of her special recipes have been refined and passed on to me by my mother.

This is one of my favorite antipasti. Large sweet peppers are baked until tender with a stuffing of sautéed eggplant, olives, tomatoes, and anchovies. They are delicious hot or at room temperature.

1 large eggplant
Salt
4 large red and/or yellow bell peppers
⅓ cup plus 2 tablespoons extra-virgin olive oil
2 medium tomatoes, peeled, seeded, and chopped
½ cup imported black olives, such as Kalamata, pitted and sliced
4 anchovy fillets, finely chopped
2 tablespoons drained capers
1 large garlic clove, peeled and finely chopped
2 tablespoons chopped flat-leaf parsley
Freshly ground black pepper
⅓ cup plus 2 teaspoons fine dry bread crumbs

1. Trim the eggplant and cut it into ¾-inch dice. Layer the pieces in a colander, sprinkling each layer lightly with salt. Place the colander on a plate and set aside to drain for about 1 hour.
2. With a small knife, cut out the stems of the peppers and remove the cores, seeds, and white membranes.
3. Preheat the oven to 450°F. Oil an 9-inch square baking pan.

4. Rinse off the salt from the eggplant cubes and pat dry with paper towels. In a large skillet, heat the ⅓ cup oil over medium heat. Add the eggplant and cook, stirring occasionally, until tender, about 10 minutes.

5. Stir in the tomatoes, olives, anchovies, capers, garlic, parsley, and pepper to taste. Bring to a simmer and cook for 5 minutes more. Stir in the ⅓ cup bread crumbs and remove from the heat.

6. Stuff the peppers with the eggplant mixture and place them in the prepared pan. Sprinkle with the remaining 2 teaspoons bread crumbs and drizzle with the remaining 2 tablespoons olive oil. Pour 1 cup of water around the peppers. Bake for 1 hour, or until tender and lightly browned. Serve warm or at room temperature.

BEEF-STUFFED PEPPERS

Peperoni Ripieni di Manzo

Serves 8

Bell peppers are made for stuffing. Not only do their shape and firm texture make them perfect containers for other foods, but their lively flavor and vibrant colors beautifully complement meat, cheese, and fish. Red peppers have the highest sugar content, so they have the sweetest and most intense flavor. Yellow peppers are slightly milder than red, and green peppers have a sharper, less mellow flavor. Any color pepper can be used in this recipe.

2 tablespoons extra-virgin olive oil
1 small onion, peeled and finely chopped
¼ cup chopped flat-leaf parsley
1 large garlic clove, peeled and finely chopped
1 pound lean ground beef
¾ cup dry red wine
2 medium tomatoes, peeled, seeded, and chopped
Salt and freshly ground black pepper
4 large red, green, or yellow bell peppers
1 large egg, lightly beaten
½ cup finely chopped prosciutto (about 2 ounces)
½ cup freshly grated Parmigiano-Reggiano
3 tablespoons dry bread crumbs

1. In a large skillet, cook the oil and the onion over medium heat until tender, about 5 minutes. Stir in the parsley and garlic. Add the beef and cook, stirring to break up any lumps, for 10 minutes or until the meat is browned.

2. Add the wine and cook until the liquid has evaporated, about 5 minutes. Stir in the tomatoes and salt and pepper to taste. Cook until thickened, about 10 minutes more. Remove from the heat and let cool slightly.

3. Preheat the oven to 350°F. Lightly oil a 12- × 9-inch baking dish.

4. Cut the peppers in half lengthwise and remove the stems and seeds. With a small knife, cut away the white membranes. Place the peppers in the prepared dish.

5. Stir the egg, prosciutto, and Parmigiano into the filling mixture. Spoon the mixture into the pepper halves. Sprinkle with the bread crumbs. Pour 1 cup of water around the peppers.

6. Bake until the peppers are tender and the crumbs are lightly browned, about 45 minutes. Serve warm or at room temperature.

TUNA-STUFFED PEPPERS

Peperoni Ripieni al Tonno

Serves 8

4 large yellow or red bell peppers

1 6½-ounce can tuna packed in olive oil, drained

2 anchovies, finely chopped

1 large tomato, finely chopped

½ cup dry bread crumbs

¼ cup imported black olives, pitted and chopped

2 tablespoons chopped flat-leaf parsley

Salt and freshly ground black pepper

¼ cup extra-virgin olive oil

1 cup dry white wine

1. Preheat the oven to 400°F. Lightly oil an 11- × 8- × 2-inch baking pan.

2. Cut the peppers in half lengthwise and remove the seeds, stems, and white membranes. Arrange the peppers cut side up in the prepared pan.

3. In a bowl, finely mash the tuna. Add the anchovies, tomato, bread crumbs, olives, parsley, and salt and pepper to taste. Stir in 2 tablespoons of the oil.

4. Fill the peppers with the mixture. Pour the wine around the peppers. Drizzle with the remaining 2 tablespoons oil. Bake for 40 minutes, or until the peppers are tender. Serve at room temperature.

STUFFED ZUCCHINI FLOWERS

Fiori di Zucchini Ripieni

Serves 4 to 6

Every time I go to Rome, I know where my first meal will be. I hurry to Da Giggetto, a trattoria in the ancient Jewish ghetto that specializes in classic Roman cooking. Spaghetti tossed with garlic, hot pepper, and the tiny, sweet clams no bigger than a thumbnail called *vongole verace* are a favorite, as are artichokes fried crispy and brown. But what I really crave is a summer specialty, stuffed zucchini flowers.

What may sound like the brainchild of some overly imaginative chef is a traditional Italian dish. I remember my mother growing zucchini plants in our tiny city garden. The zucchini were fine but what we really waited for were the zucchini flowers.

When they appeared, mom would show my sister and me how to tell which ones would form a zucchini and which would not. If you grow your own zucchini, examine the stems of the flowers. Those that will produce a zucchini have stems that actually are miniature squash. Those with narrow green stems will not bear fruit, so you may as well pick them and turn them into something delicious. The flowers are at their best when they are not fully opened.

If you aren't a gardener, you can sometimes find zucchini and other squash blossoms at farmer's markets and specialty produce shops. Or ask a gardening friend to pick some for you. The flowers don't last very long, so plan to use them the same day they are picked.

24 large zucchini or other squash flowers (about ¼ pound)
1¼ cups all-purpose flour
½ teaspoon salt
⅛ teaspoon baking powder
Freshly ground black pepper

1 cup cold water

1 2-ounce can anchovy fillets, drained

**2 ounces mozzarella, cut into 1- × ¼- × ¼-inch
sticks (you should have 24)**

Vegetable oil for deep frying

1. Gently spread open the petals of each squash flower and pinch out the stamen. Holding a flower by its stem, quickly dip one at a time into a bowl of cold water. Pat the flowers dry and place them open end down on a towel to drain.

2. In a medium bowl, combine the flour, salt, baking powder, and pepper to taste. Add the water and stir just until smooth. Set aside.

3. Pat the anchovies dry with paper towels. Cut each crosswise into 3 pieces. Insert a piece of anchovy fillet and a stick of mozzarella in each flower. Pinch the flower petals closed and twist the ends slightly to seal.

4. Fill a deep fryer with oil according to the manufacturer's recommendation or pour 1 inch of oil into a deep heavy skillet. Heat the oil to 375°F on a deep-frying thermometer.

5. Stir the batter and carefully dip the flowers in it to coat thoroughly. Drain off excess batter. Fry the flowers in batches, turning them, until they are golden on all sides, about 4 minutes. With a slotted spoon, transfer the flowers to paper towels to drain. Serve immediately.

SAUSAGE-STUFFED TOMATOES

Pomodori Ripieni di Salsiccia

Serves 6

Fresh Italian sausages are a delicious filling for fat, ripe tomatoes. If possible, buy sausages at a market that makes its own with lean pork and a minimum of spices. If you cannot find sausages with fennel seeds, add about ½ teaspoon seeds to the sausage mixture when sautéing the meat.

6 medium ripe, but not soft, tomatoes
8 ounces sweet Italian sausages with fennel,
 casings removed
1 large onion, peeled and chopped
1 garlic clove, peeled and chopped
¼ cup plus 1 tablespoon freshly grated
 Parmigiano-Reggiano
¼ cup dry bread crumbs
¼ cup chopped fresh basil
Salt and freshly ground black pepper

1. Preheat the oven to 350°F. Oil a 9-inch square baking pan.
2. Slice the tops from the tomatoes. With a knife or serrated grapefruit spoon scoop out the seeds and pulp; discard the seeds and chop the pulp. Place the shells in the prepared pan.
3. In a medium skillet, cook the sausage for 5 minutes, stirring to break up. Add the onion and garlic. Cook until the sausage is browned and the onion is tender, about 10 minutes. Stir in the tomato pulp and simmer for 10 to 15 minutes, or until the tomato juices have evaporated. Remove from the heat. Stir in the ¼ cup cheese, the bread crumbs, basil, and salt and pepper to taste.
4. Spoon the mixture into the tomato shells. Sprinkle with the remaining 1 tablespoon cheese. Bake for 25 minutes, or until lightly browned. Serve warm.

BEANS

I Fagioli

Beans, like tomatoes, corn, and peppers, came to Italy and the rest of Europe only after the discovery of America. Before that time, the only bean that was available was the fava, a diet staple since prehistoric times. Italians now eat all kinds of beans in soups, pasta, salads, as side dishes, in sauces, and in risotto.

Beans are even sold as snacks and street food. In Rome's Borghese Gardens an elderly black-clad woman sells large, fat beans called *lupini* soaked in brine (as well as an assortment of olives) from plastic buckets on her homemade cart. With each order, she shapes a cone from a piece of glossy magazine paper and pours in the beans. Customers peel the beans and nibble them as they stroll among the chestnut trees in the beautiful old park.

Fiorentin

mangia fagioli,

lecca piatti

e tovaglioli.

The Florentine

eats beans,

licks the plates

and tablecloths.

TUSCAN-STYLE BEANS

Fagioli alla Toscana

Serves 10 to 12
Makes about 6 cups

Tuscans love beans in every form and eat them so often that their countrymen refer to them as *mangiafagioli*, bean-eaters. Simply cooked and drizzled with olive oil or added to salads, soups, or stews, Tuscan beans are invariably tender and creamy. The secret is to oven-bake the beans slowly and carefully, which tenderizes them and retains their shape.

When cooking any type of dried beans, don't be tempted to raise the heat or to add salt or acidic ingredients until the beans are fully cooked. These ingredients would cause the skins of the beans to toughen and no matter how long you cooked them, they would remain hard. Add them at the end of the cooking time, when the beans are tender.

Fagioli alla Toscana can be served as is or used in other recipes calling for cooked beans. Try spooning them over Bruschetta (page 152) with a drizzle of extra-virgin olive oil and thin slices of red onion. Other varieties of dried beans can be cooked this way, though the cooking times will vary.

1 pound dried cannellini or Great Northern beans
1 large garlic clove, peeled
1 sprig fresh sage
Salt
Extra-virgin olive oil
Freshly ground black pepper

1. Rinse the beans and remove any small stones or shriveled beans. Place the beans in a bowl with cold water to cover by 2 inches. Refrigerate for at least 4 hours or overnight.
2. Preheat the oven to 300°F.
3. Drain the beans and place them in a flameproof casserole with a cover. Add fresh water to cover by 1 inch. Add the garlic, sage,

and 1 tablespoon olive oil, cover, and bring just to a simmer over low heat.

4. Place the casserole in the oven and cook until the beans are very tender, about 45 minutes to 1 hour. (Cooking times may vary as much as 30 minutes.)

5. Add salt to taste and cook 5 minutes more. Just before serving, drain the beans. Serve warm or at room temperature with extra-virgin olive oil and freshly ground pepper to taste.

VENETIAN-STYLE BEANS

Fagioli alla Veneta

Serves 4 to 6

Anchovy fillets give many Venetian dishes a distinctive flavor, including these tasty beans. Canned beans can be substituted for home-cooked beans if necessary.

1 garlic clove, peeled and finely chopped
2 tablespoons extra-virgin olive oil
5 anchovy fillets
2 tablespoons red wine vinegar
2 tablespoons chopped flat-leaf parsley
Freshly ground black pepper
2½ cups drained cooked cannellini beans (see page 74) or 1 19-ounce can cannellini beans, drained and rinsed

1. In a medium skillet, cook the garlic in the olive oil over medium-low heat until golden.

2. Stir in the anchovies, vinegar, parsley, and pepper to taste. Cook 3 minutes. Stir in the beans and cook just until heated through. Serve warm or at room temperature.

BEANS WITH FENNEL SEED

Fagioli con Semi di Finocchio

Serves 10 to 12
Makes about 6 cups

Fennel-flavored beans are great with pork.

1 pound dried cannellini or Great Northern beans
1 medium onion, peeled
1 medium celery rib, trimmed
1 medium carrot, trimmed
2 garlic cloves, peeled and lightly crushed
1 teaspoon fennel seeds
Salt
Extra-virgin olive oil
Freshly ground black pepper

1. Place the beans in a large bowl with cold water to cover by about 2 inches. Refrigerate for at least 4 hours or overnight.
2. Preheat the oven to 300°F.
3. Drain the beans and place them in a 6-quart flameproof casserole with a cover. Add fresh water to cover by 1 inch. Add the onion, celery, carrot, garlic, and fennel seeds, cover, and bring just to a simmer over low heat.
4. Place the casserole in the oven and cook until the beans are very tender, 45 minutes to 1 hour. Add salt to taste and simmer 5 minutes more. (Cooking times may vary as much as 30 minutes.)
5. Remove and discard the onion, celery, carrot, and garlic. Just before serving, drain the beans. Drizzle them with oil and season with a generous grinding of pepper. Serve warm or at room temperature.

LENTIL SALAD

Insalata di Lenticchie

Serves 8

When I was little, I refused to eat lentils, and now I can't imagine why, since they are so delicious. On a cold winter day, I crave a warming lentil soup, but this salad is good any time of the year.

8 ounces lentils, rinsed
1 small onion, peeled
1 bay leaf
Salt
½ cup shredded carrot (about 1 large)
¼ cup finely chopped red onion
¼ cup finely chopped flat-leaf parsley
1 garlic clove, peeled and finely chopped
Freshly ground black pepper
¼ cup extra-virgin olive oil
2 tablespoons red wine vinegar

1. Combine the lentils, whole onion, bay leaf, and 5 cups water in a medium saucepan. Bring to a simmer over low heat. Cover and cook for 45 minutes or until the lentils are tender but not mushy. Five minutes before the lentils are done, add salt to taste. Drain, and remove the onion and bay leaf.
2. In a large bowl, combine the lentils with the carrot, chopped red onion, parsley, garlic, and pepper to taste. Stir in the olive oil and vinegar. Chill for at least 1 hour before serving. Taste for seasoning and serve.

FAVA BEANS WITH PROSCIUTTO AND PARMESAN

Fave con Prosciutto e Parmigiano

Serves 4

In Rome, fava beans are a harbinger of spring and the arrival of the first slim green beans of the year is an occasion for celebration. In restaurants, favas are served raw, still in their pods. Diners shell the beans and eat them with shards of salty Pecorino cheese, a delicious combination, especially when washed down with some of the local chilled Frascati.

Fava beans, also known as broad beans, are not as well known here, which is surprising, because they have been a staple of Mediterranean and Middle Eastern cooking for centuries.

Too often, fava beans are overly mature when they are harvested and the skins have become tough and the beans starchy. When buying fava beans, choose those with firm green pods, the smaller the better. Snap the pods open and you will find the beans nestled in a plush nest that looks like styrofoam. Remove the beans and discard the pods.

Some cooks feel that it is necessary to peel off the skin that covers each bean, but this can be tedious; if the beans are young and tender, it should not be necessary. If you want to remove the skins, blanch the beans for one minute in boiling water. Cool them under cold running water and peel off the outer skin. One pound of favas in the pod will yield about 1 cup beans.

3 pounds fresh fava beans, shelled
Salt
2 ounces sliced prosciutto, cut into thin strips (about ½ cup)
2 tablespoons extra-virgin olive oil
1½ tablespoons fresh lemon juice, or more to taste

Freshly ground black pepper
2-inch chunk of Parmigiano-Reggiano

1. In a large pot, bring 2 quarts of water to a boil over medium-high heat. Add the beans and salt to taste. Cook until tender, about 1 to 2 minutes. Drain the beans and cool under cold running water. Pat dry.

2. Place the beans and prosciutto in a bowl. In a small bowl, whisk together the oil, lemon juice, and a pinch of salt and pepper. Add to the beans and toss to coat. Taste for seasoning and add additional lemon juice or salt if desired.

3. With a vegetable peeler, shave the cheese into very thin slices. Just before serving, scatter the cheese over the beans. Serve at room temperature.

SAUTÉED FAVA BEANS
WITH PANCETTA

Fave con Pancetta

Serves 4

In the spring, I love to go to Da Giggetto Restaurant in Rome's ancient Jewish quarter for a big plate of fresh fava beans sautéed with *guanciale*, a tender cured pork product similar to pancetta. With rough country bread, these beans make a satisfying yet simple meal.

1 small onion, peeled and finely chopped
3 tablespoons extra-virgin olive oil
3 thick slices of pancetta (about 4 ounces), cut into ½-inch cubes
4 pounds fresh fava beans, shelled
1 garlic clove, peeled and finely chopped
½ teaspoon salt
Freshly ground black pepper

1. In a large saucepan, cook the onion in the olive oil over medium heat until tender, about 5 minutes.
2. Stir in the pancetta and cook 5 minutes.
3. Add the fava beans, garlic, salt, and pepper to taste. Cover and cook over low heat until the beans are tender, about 5 minutes.
4. Uncover and cook, stirring frequently, until the beans and pancetta are lightly browned, about 5 minutes. Serve hot.

BLACK-EYED PEAS WITH TOMATOES AND SAGE

Fagioli all'Uccelletto

Serves 8

"All'Uccelletto" means that these beans are made the way little birds are cooked, with tomatoes, garlic, and sage.

1 pound dried black-eyed peas, rinsed
¼ cup extra-virgin olive oil
2 large garlic cloves, peeled and finely chopped
2 medium tomatoes, peeled, seeded, and chopped
2 tablespoons chopped fresh sage
Salt and freshly ground black pepper

1. Place the peas in a large bowl with cold water to cover. Refrigerate for at least 4 hours or overnight. Drain the peas and rinse well.

2. Preheat the oven to 300°F.

3. Place the peas in a large flameproof casserole with a cover. Add water to cover by 1 inch. Bring to a simmer over low heat. Cover the casserole and place it in the oven. Bake for about 1 hour or until the peas are very tender.

4. Meanwhile, in a large saucepan, heat the olive oil. Add the garlic and cook over medium heat for 1 minute, or until golden. Add the tomatoes, sage, and salt and pepper to taste. Simmer for 20 minutes.

5. Drain the peas and add them to the tomatoes. Simmer for 15 minutes. Serve warm.

CHICK-PEA—FLOUR FRITTERS

Panelle

Serves 8 to 10

Panelle are a kind of typical Sicilian street food sold at sidewalk stands and shops that feature fried foods called *friggitorie*. The fritters can be eaten as is or made into a sandwich.

At Joe's Focacceria on Avenue U in Brooklyn, panelle sandwiches are served on a split sesame seed bun. Several layers of panelle are stacked on the bottom half, then topped with a thick layer of ricotta and a sprinkling of grated Pecorino. The open sandwich is baked briefly to heat the cheeses and toast the bread, then closed just before serving.

Chick-pea flour can be purchased in many Italian groceries. Do not use the widely available Indian chick-pea flour; the flavor and texture are completely different.

1¾ cups chick-pea flour (½ pound)
½ teaspoon salt
Freshly ground black pepper
3 cups cold water
¼ cup freshly grated Pecorino Romano or
  Parmigiano-Reggiano
2 tablespoons finely chopped flat-leaf parsley
Vegetable oil for frying

1. Line a 6-cup loaf pan with plastic wrap.

2. In a large heavy saucepan, combine the chick-pea flour, salt, pepper to taste, and water. Stir well. Bring to a boil and cook over medium-low heat, stirring constantly, until the mixture is very thick and pulls away from the side of the pan. Stir in the cheese and parsley.

3. Pour the hot mixture into the prepared loaf pan. Tap the pan on the countertop to settle the mixture. Cover and refrigerate until firm, at least several hours or overnight.

4. Remove the chick-pea mixture from the pan and place it on a cutting board. With a sharp knife, cut the loaf into ¼-inch slices. Cut each slice in half.

5. Fill a deep fryer with oil according to the manufacturer's instructions or pour ¾ inch oil into a large heavy skillet. Heat until the temperature of the oil reaches 375°F on a deep-frying thermometer.

6. Fry the panelle a few at a time, turning once, for 3 to 5 minutes or until golden brown and slightly puffed. Drain on paper towels. Serve the panelle hot or at room temperature. (Panelle may be made ahead and set aside at room temperature. Reheat for 10 minutes in a 350°F oven if desired.)

BEANS, BROCCOLI RABE, AND GARLIC

Fagioli, Broccoli Rabe, e
Aglio

Serves 6

Broccoli rabe goes by many different names. I have seen it labeled broccoli or broccoletto di rape, raab, or rabe, or rapini. Oriental markets sell a similar vegetable called choy sum or Chinese broccoli.

Whatever you call it, it is a bitter, pungent vegetable that may take some getting used to. Boiling the vegetable helps to tame the flavor as well as retain the bright green color.

The amount of garlic in this recipe is up to the cook. Since the garlic is sautéed gently and left whole, the flavor is not overwhelming. In fact, it makes a subtle flavor bridge between the broccoli rabe and the beans.

1 pound broccoli rabe
Salt
6 large garlic cloves (or more or less to taste),
  peeled
½ cup extra-virgin olive oil
¼ teaspoon crushed red pepper
2½ cups drained cooked cannellini beans (see
  page 74) or 1 19-ounce can cannellini beans,
  rinsed and drained.

1. Rinse the broccoli rabe in cold water and drain it well. Discard any bruised leaves or stems. Cut off the stem ends and scrape the lower part of the stalks with a paring knife. Cut the broccoli rabe into 1-inch lengths.
2. Bring a large pot of water to a boil. Add the broccoli rabe and salt to taste. Cook, uncovered, until the broccoli rabe is tender, about 5 minutes. Drain well.

3. In a large skillet, heat the garlic and olive oil over low heat. Cook until the garlic is golden on all sides, about 5 minutes. Stir in the red pepper.

4. Add the beans and stir them to coat with the oil. Stir in the broccoli rabe and ½ teaspoon salt. Cook, stirring gently, until hot, about 3 minutes. Serve warm or at room temperature.

BEAN AND SALAMI SALAD

Insalata di Fagioli con Salame

Serves 4

The neutral flavor of beans makes them a perfect foil for spicy ingredients like salami and pickled peppers. You can use sweet peppers, either homemade (page 113) or store-bought, or, for a spicier salad, pickled peperoncini.

2½ cups drained cooked cannellini beans (see page 74) or 1 19-ounce can cannellini beans, drained and rinsed
¼ cup chopped flat-leaf parsley
¼ cup finely chopped red onion
⅓ cup drained pickled peppers, cut into thin strips
4 thin slices salami, cut into thin strips (about ¼ cup)
2 tablespoons extra-virgin olive oil
1½ tablespoons red wine vinegar
Salt and freshly ground black pepper

1. In a bowl, combine the beans, parsley, onion, peppers, and salami.

2. In a small bowl, whisk together the oil, vinegar, and salt and pepper to taste. Pour over the bean mixture and toss well. Chill slightly before serving.

SALADS AND PICKLED VEGETABLES

Insalate e Sott'Aceti

~~~~~~~~~~~~~~~~~~~~

L'insalata va

preparata da

chi è più pazzo

in casa.

~~~~~~~~

Salad should be

prepared by the

craziest person

in the house.

Italians use only the simplest of salad dressings. Extra-virgin olive oil, a low-acid red or white wine vinegar or fresh lemon juice, and salt and pepper are the only ingredients—a far cry from the stuff sold in bottles as Italian dressing. Instead of masking flavors, the dressing is intended to enhance the vegetables and other foods with which it is served. The flavor comes from the combination of vegetables and other ingredients that are tossed with the dressing.

In most cases, these salads are best when freshly made. They should be served at room temperature or at most lightly chilled for the fullest flavor. Always taste salads that have been marinated before serving them, as the seasonings can be absorbed and a few drops of vinegar or lemon juice may be needed to perk up the flavor.

Many vegetables, such as mushrooms, onions, peppers, and artichokes, can be preserved in vinegar or in olive oil. They add a spicy accent note to antipasti and go well with cheeses, cold meats, grilled vegetables, and frittatas.

ARTICHOKE AND PARMESAN SALAD

Insalata di Carciofi e Parmigiano

Serves 4

Italians grow a spineless variety of artichoke that is so tender it can be served uncooked in salads. American artichokes need to be well trimmed and lightly cooked to tenderize them. The artichokes can be prepared several hours ahead of time but dress the salad just before serving.

2 lemons
4 medium artichokes
Salt
¼ cup fruity olive oil
Freshly ground black pepper
4-ounce piece Parmigiano-Reggiano, at room temperature

1. Squeeze the juice of 1 of the lemons into a bowl filled with cold water.
2. Beginning near the base of each artichoke, bend the leaves back one at a time, snapping off the upper green portion and leaving the lower pale green or whitish portion of each leaf intact. When only a central cone of leaves remains, slice off the top 1 inch. With a small knife, pare away the green leaf ends around the base of the artichoke. Trim about ¼ inch off the stem end and pare away the tough outer layer of the stem. Drop each artichoke into the bowl of lemon water to prevent it from turning brown while you prepare the remaining artichokes.
3. Bring a large saucepan of water to a boil. Drain the artichokes and add them to the boiling water with salt to taste. Cover and cook over medium-low heat for 30 to 40 minutes or until the artichoke hearts are tender when pierced with a knife. Drain well. When cool

enough to handle, cut each artichoke in half lengthwise and scoop out the choke with a small knife. Cut each half into thin lengthwise slices.

4. Squeeze 3 tablespoons juice from the remaining lemon. In a large bowl, whisk together the lemon juice, olive oil, ¼ teaspoon salt, and a generous amount of black pepper. Gently stir in the artichoke slices. Divide the artichokes among four plates. With a vegetable peeler, shave the Parmigiano into thin slices. Scatter the cheese over the artichokes. Serve immediately.

ORANGE AND ARTICHOKE SALAD

Insalata di Arance e Carciofi

Serves 4

Sicily is noted for its excellent citrus fruits. Naturally, the Sicilians have many creative uses for them, such as this unusual salad.

2 medium artichokes
1 lemon
2 large navel oranges
¼ cup sliced pitted imported black olives, such as Kalamata
¼ cup finely chopped red onion
¼ cup extra-virgin olive oil
Salt and freshly ground black pepper

1. Prepare the artichokes, using the juice of the lemon, through step 3 as directed on page 88.
2. Peel the oranges, removing all of the white pith. Cut the oranges into sections, avoiding the white membrane.
3. Place the orange wedges, artichoke slices, olives, and onion in a bowl. Drizzle with the oil and sprinkle with salt and pepper to taste. Toss gently. Serve immediately.

ORANGE, PARMESAN, AND WALNUT SALAD

Insalata di Arancia, Parmigiano, e Noci

Serves 4

I first had this salad at a little trattoria in Milan, where it was made with *tarocchi*, the tart blood oranges with deep red flesh and juice that appear in Italian markets from December to February. Occasionally I can find blood oranges in my local market, but at a stiff price. Navel oranges can be substituted, with a little bit of fresh lemon juice to cut the sweetness.

½ **cup walnut pieces**
3 **navel oranges**
1 **teaspoon fresh lemon juice**
3 **tablespoons extra-virgin olive oil**
Salt and freshly ground black pepper
1 **small head radicchio, torn into bite-size pieces**
2-**ounce chunk of Parmigiano-Reggiano, cut into slivers (about ¼ cup)**

1. Preheat the oven to 350°F. Spread the nuts on a baking sheet and bake for 10 minutes or until lightly toasted. Let cool.
2. Squeeze 3 tablespoons juice from 1 of the oranges. In a small bowl, combine the orange juice, lemon juice, olive oil, and salt and pepper to taste.
3. Peel the remaining oranges, removing all of the white pith. Cut the oranges into sections, avoiding the membranes.
4. In a bowl, combine the radicchio, oranges, and walnuts. Add the dressing and toss gently. Sprinkle with the cheese. Serve immediately.

RAW VEGETABLES WITH OLIVE OIL

Pinzimonio

Serves 4

Italians rarely eat food with their fingers—fresh fruit and pizza, for example, are always eaten with a knife and fork. But pinzimonio is an exception. Pinzimonio are raw vegetables that are dipped into seasoned extra-virgin olive oil. The name is derived from the Italian word for pincers, since the vegetables are picked up with finger and thumb.

Use any seasonal vegetables that taste good raw. Wash the vegetables well and trim them, but leave them whole or in large pieces. For the most dramatic presentation, arrange the vegetables like a bouquet of flowers in a glass bowl.

2 red, yellow, or green bell peppers, cored, seeded, and cut into ½-inch strips
4 tender celery ribs with leaves intact
4 thin carrots, peeled and trimmed
1 fennel bulb, trimmed and quartered
4 scallions, roots trimmed
1 head endive, leaves separated
4 radishes, trimmed
6 to 8 ice cubes
About 1 cup extra-virgin olive oil
Coarse salt
Black pepper (in a mill)

1. Arrange the vegetables decoratively in a bowl. Scatter the ice cubes among the vegetables for extra crispness.
2. Provide each guest with a small bowl of oil. Pass the salt and pepper separately so each guest can season the oil to taste.

REINFORCEMENT SALAD

Insalata di Rinforzo

Serves 6 to 8

This salad is typically prepared in Neapolitan homes for Christmas Eve as an accompaniment to the multicourse fish dinner that is served on that night. After Christmas, additional ingredients are added daily to "reinforce" the salad so it will last until the Epiphany on January 6. Each new addition makes it taste better and better.

Insalata di Rinforzo is ideal to have on hand for impromptu meals. It goes especially well with cold meats and, of course, seafood.

1 medium cauliflower (about 1½ pounds)
Salt
1½ cups thinly sliced tender celery
½ cup chopped pitted green olives
½ cup chopped pitted black olives
½ cup pickled sweet red peppers, cut into thin strips
4 peperoncini or other mildly hot pickled peppers, seeded and chopped (about ¼ cup)
1 tablespoon drained capers
¼ cup extra-virgin olive oil
¼ cup white wine vinegar

1. Cut the cauliflower into bite-size florets. Bring a large pot of water to a boil. Add the cauliflower and salt to taste. Cook over medium heat until the cauliflower is tender yet still crisp when pierced with a knife, about 5 minutes. Drain the cauliflower and cool under cold running water.

2. In a bowl, combine the cauliflower with all the remaining ingredients and toss well. Cover and refrigerate overnight. Let stand at room temperature for about 30 minutes before serving. Toss gently and taste and correct the seasoning.

GRILLED VEGETABLE SALAD

Insalata di Verdure alla Griglia

Serves 6

2 medium eggplants (about 1 pound each)
Salt
1¼ pounds plum tomatoes
½ cup shredded fresh basil or flat-leaf parsley
2 garlic cloves, peeled and chopped
½ cup extra-virgin olive oil
2 tablespoons red wine vinegar
Freshly ground black pepper
2 large red bell peppers

1. Trim the eggplants and cut them into slices about ½ inch thick. Layer the slices in a colander, sprinkling each layer lightly with salt. Place the colander on a plate and drain for about 1 hour.

2. Prepare a fire in a barbecue grill or preheat the broiler.

3. Place the tomatoes on the grill and cook, turning frequently with tongs, until the skin is lightly charred and loosened. Remove the tomatoes and let cool slightly. Slip off the tomato skins and cut out the stem ends. Place the tomatoes in a bowl and mash them with a fork. Stir in the basil, garlic, ¼ cup of the olive oil, the vinegar, and salt and pepper to taste.

4. Place the peppers on the grill and cook, turning occasionally, until they are charred and the skin is blistered. Remove the peppers and let cool slightly. Peel the peppers and remove the stems and seeds. Cut the peppers into narrow strips. Add them to the tomatoes.

5. Rinse off the salt from the eggplant slices and pat dry with paper towels. Brush the slices with the remaining ¼ cup olive oil. Place on the grill and cook, turning once, until lightly browned and tender. Remove the slices and let cool slightly. Cut the slices into ½-inch strips. Add them to the peppers and tomatoes. Toss to mix. Serve at room temperature.

SICILIAN EGGPLANT SALAD

Caponata

Serves 8

No one in Italy knows more ways to cook eggplant than the Sicilians, but this just might be the best.

Frying the eggplant in a large quantity of hot oil sears it and prevents it from soaking up more oil than is necessary. Cooked this way, eggplant will actually absorb less oil than if sautéed.

The flavors of caponata need to mellow overnight in the refrigerator, so it can be a prepared 1 to 3 days in advance.

3 medium eggplants (about 1 pound each)
Salt
Vegetable oil for frying
3 tablespoons extra-virgin olive oil
2 large onions, peeled and chopped
4 celery ribs, chopped
1 28-ounce can Italian peeled tomatoes
1½ cups chopped pitted green olives
1 3½-ounce jar capers, drained and chopped
3 tablespoons sugar
¼ cup red wine vinegar

1. Trim the eggplants and cut into 1-inch cubes. Layer the cubes in a large colander, sprinkling each layer with salt. Place the colander over a plate and let stand for 1 hour. Rinse off the salt under cool water and pat the eggplant dry.

2. In a deep heavy skillet, heat 1 inch of vegetable oil until the temperature reaches 375°F on a deep-frying thermometer. Add about one quarter of the eggplant and cook, turning, until browned on all sides, about 5 minutes. Remove the eggplant with a slotted spoon and place on absorbent paper to drain. Repeat with the remaining eggplant.

3. In a large saucepan, heat the olive oil over medium heat. Add the onions and celery and cook for 5 minutes, or until softened. Stir in the tomatoes and cook for 10 minutes. Stir in the olives and capers and cook until the sauce is thick, about 10 minutes more. Stir in the eggplant, sugar, and vinegar and cook for 10 minutes. Let cool and refrigerate overnight. Serve at room temperature. This can be refrigerated for up to 1 week.

ZUCCHINI AND PARMESAN SALAD

Carpaccio di Zucchini

Serves 4

Faith Willinger is the author of an indispensable guidebook for travelers and stay-at-homes alike called *Eating in Italy* (Hearst, 1989). One day she surprised me with this simple yet amazingly good combination of raw zucchini and Parmigiano. Faith sometimes substitutes balsamic vinegar for the lemon juice.

8 ounces small zucchini
3 tablespoons fresh lemon juice
⅓ cup extra-virgin olive oil
Salt and freshly ground black pepper
About 2 ounces Parmigiano-Reggiano, in 1 piece

1. With a vegetable brush, scrub the zucchini well under cold running water. Trim off the ends.
2. In a food processor or on a mandoline, slice the zucchini very thin. Arrange the slices, overlapping them slightly, on a shallow platter.
3. In a small bowl, whisk together the lemon juice, olive oil, and salt and pepper to taste until blended. Drizzle over the zucchini.
4. With a vegetable peeler, shave the Parmigiano into thin slices. Scatter the slices over the zucchini. Serve immediately.

WARM CHEESE SALAD

Insalata di Formaggio Caldo

Serves 4

Scamorza is a dried mozzarella cheese. If it is not available, substitute provola dolce (mild provolone) or an aged Swiss cheese.

1 bunch arugula, stems removed
1 small radicchio
1 small Boston lettuce
5 tablespoons extra-virgin olive oil
8 ounces scamorza or provola dolce, cut into 8 slices
½ teaspoon dried oregano
1 tablespoon balsamic vinegar
Salt and freshly ground black pepper

1. Wash the arugula, radicchio, and lettuce well. Dry them in a salad spinner. Tear the radicchio and lettuce into bite-size pieces. You should have about 6 cups of greens.
2. Preheat the oven to 450°F. Brush a baking sheet with some of the olive oil.
3. Arrange the cheese on the prepared baking sheet. Sprinkle with oregano.
4. Just before serving, whisk together the remaining oil, the vinegar, and salt and pepper to taste. Toss the greens with the dressing. Arrange the greens on four plates.
5. Bake the cheese just until it is warm and beginning to melt, about 1 minute. With a spatula, slide 2 slices of cheese onto each salad. Serve immediately.

MUSHROOM AND PARMIGIANO SALAD

Insalata di Funghi e Parmigiano

Serves 4

Nutty cheese, crunchy vegetables, and tender mushrooms make a light and refreshing salad combination—definitely one of my favorites. During the warm months this salad is often served as a main course and fresh porcini or other wild mushrooms are frequently substitued for the cultivated mushrooms.

2-ounce piece Parmigiano-Reggiano, at room temperature
2 tender celery ribs, trimmed and thinly sliced
1 medium carrot, peeled, trimmed, and shredded
8 ounces white mushrooms, trimmed and thinly sliced
⅓ cup extra-virgin olive oil, or more to taste
4 teaspoons fresh lemon juice, or more to taste
Salt and freshly ground black pepper

1. With a vegetable peeler, shave the Parmigiano into paper-thin slices. Set aside.

2. In a large bowl, combine the celery, carrot, and mushrooms. In a small bowl, whisk together the olive oil, lemon juice, and salt and pepper to taste. Pour the dressing over the vegetables and toss well. Taste for seasoning and add additional oil and lemon juice if desired.

3. Divide the vegetables among four salad plates. Top with the cheese. Serve immediately.

POTATO SALAD ARTUSI

Insalata di Patate di Artusi

Serves 6 to 8

Pellegrino Artusi authored what is probably Italy's most famous cookbook, *La scienza in cucina e l'arte di mangiar bene* (*Science in the Kitchen and the Art of Eating Well*), familiarly called "Artusi." It was first published in 1891 and is still in print, with more than one million copies sold. Though instructions are sketchy and no quantities are given, it makes good reading and many of the recipes are still fresh and appealing.

One recipe that I found particularly appetizing is this salad of potatoes and celery flavored with sweet red pepper, salty anchovies, and capers. It is as attractive as it is delicious.

1½ pounds new potatoes
Salt
1 cup sliced celery
½ cup chopped red bell pepper
¼ cup chopped red onion
8 anchovy fillets, chopped
2 tablespoons capers, drained and chopped
¼ cup extra-virgin olive oil
2 tablespoons white wine vinegar
½ teaspoon dried oregano
Freshly ground black pepper

1. Place the potatoes in a medium saucepan and add cold water to cover and salt to taste. Cover and bring to a simmer over medium heat. Cook until the potatoes are tender when pierced with a knife, about 20 minutes. Drain well. Let cool slightly. Cut into ¼-inch slices.

2. In a bowl, combine the potatoes, celery, red pepper, onion, anchovies, and capers.

3. In a small bowl, whisk together the olive oil, vinegar, oregano, and salt and pepper to taste. Pour over the vegetables and toss gently. Cover and chill briefly before serving. This can be made 1 day in advance.

POTATO AND ARUGULA SALAD

Insalata di Arugula e Patate

Serves 4 to 6

1 pound new potatoes
Salt
½ cup finely chopped red onion
¼ cup extra-virgin olive oil
1 tablespoon white wine vinegar
Freshly ground black pepper
1 bunch arugula, washed, dried, trimmed, and
** torn into bite-size pieces (about 2 cups)**

1. Place the potatoes in a medium saucepan and add cold water to cover and salt to taste. Cover and bring to a simmer over medium heat. Cook until tender when pierced with a knife, about 20 minutes. Drain. Let cool slightly, then peel and dice the potatoes.

2. In a bowl, combine the potatoes and onion.

3. In a small bowl, whisk the oil and vinegar with salt and pepper to taste. Pour over the potatoes and onion and toss well. Let cool completely.

4. Stir in the arugula. Taste for seasoning. Serve at room temperature.

POTATO AND SCALLION SALAD

Insalata di Patate e Scalogna

Serves 6 to 8

This salad is so simple that I hesitated to include it, but it is so delicious that I could not bear to leave it out. It illustrates perfectly exquisite simplicity and earthy goodness, the two elements of Italian cooking.

2 pounds new potatoes, peeled
Salt
½ cup finely chopped scallions
⅓ cup extra-virgin olive oil
Freshly ground black pepper

1. Places the potatoes in a large saucepan and add cold water to cover and salt to taste. Cover and bring to a simmer over medium heat. Cook until the potatoes are tender when pierced with a knife, about 20 minutes. Drain the potatoes, let cool slightly, and cut them into ½-inch dice.

2. In a bowl, combine the potatoes, scallions, olive oil, and salt and pepper to taste. Toss gently. Serve warm or at room temperature. This can be refrigerated overnight.

ROASTED PEPPER AND MOZZARELLA SALAD

Insalata di Peperoni e Mozzarella

Serves 6

Sweet roasted peppers have a natural affinity for salty foods like cheese. They go particularly well with fresh mozzarella or a piquant cheese such as ricotta salata or provolone.

This beautiful salad is also good made with fresh basil or parsley instead of the oregano. Be sure to provide lots of good bread to soak up the marinade juices.

6 red, green, or yellow bell peppers, roasted, peeled, and seeded (see pages 30–33), with their juices
2 large garlic cloves, peeled and cut into slivers
2 tablespoons chopped drained capers
1 tablespoon chopped fresh oregano or 1 teaspoon dried
Salt and freshly ground black pepper
⅓ cup extra-virgin olive oil
8 ounces fresh mozzarella, cut into ¼-inch slices

1. Cut the peppers into 1-inch strips.
2. In a bowl, combine all the ingredients except the mozzarella. Cover and marinate at room temperature for at least 1 hour.
3. Place the mozzarella slices, overlapping them slightly, on a serving platter. Spoon the peppers and their juices onto the platter beside the cheese.

BELGIAN ENDIVE SALAD IN THE STYLE OF PUNTARELLE

Insalata di Indivia uso Puntarelle

Serves 4

In Rome, early spring is the time to eat *insalata di puntarelle*. The tender shoots of a chicory-like vegetable, puntarelle are first soaked in cold water, which causes them to curl up. This recipe comes from Da Giggetto, which, like most Roman trattorias, serves puntarelle with a distinctive garlic and anchovy dressing. Whole families arrive to eat bowls full of the salad, which is considered something of a spring tonic.

Unfortunately, puntarelle are not available here. But Belgian endive, though not curly, makes a good stand-in.

3 medium heads Belgian endive
4 anchovy fillets, chopped
1 garlic clove, peeled and minced
3 tablespoons extra-virgin olive oil
1½ tablespoons red wine vinegar
Salt and freshly ground black pepper

1. Cut the endive in half lengthwise and remove the central core. Rinse in cool water and dry well. Cut crosswise into ¼-inch strips and place in a bowl.

2. In a small bowl, mash the anchovies and garlic with a wooden spoon to form a paste. Whisk in the oil, vinegar, and salt and pepper to taste.

3. Pour the dressing over the endive and toss well. Serve immediately.

GREEN BEAN SALAD WITH POTATOES AND MINT

Fagiolini con Patate e Menta

Serves 4 to 6

Another old family recipe, one that goes nicely with fish or meat antipasti.

12 ounces new potatoes, scrubbed
1 pound green beans
Salt
½ cup chopped fresh mint
½ cup extra-virgin olive oil
3 tablespoons red wine vinegar
Freshly ground black pepper
½ cup thinly sliced red onion

1. Cut the potatoes into ¼-inch-thick slices, then cut the slices into ¼-inch-thick sticks. Trim the beans and cut them into 2-inch lengths.

2. In a large saucepan, bring 4 quarts of water to a boil. Add the potatoes and salt to taste. When the water returns to a boil, add the beans. Cook until the vegetables are tender, 5 to 8 minutes. Drain well and cool under cold running water.

3. In a shallow serving bowl, whisk together the mint, oil, vinegar, and salt and pepper to taste. Add the potatoes, beans, and onions; stir well to coat. Let marinate for 1 hour, stirring occasionally. Taste for seasoning. Do not refrigerate.

TUNA AND GREEN BEAN SALAD

Insalata di Tonno e Fagiolini

Serves 6

Green beans keep their bright color best when cooked uncovered in a large pot of boiling water. If you cook them ahead, wrap them in a kitchen towel and hold them at room temperature. Chilling alters the flavor and makes the cooked beans taste flat and stale.

1 pound green beans, trimmed
Salt
¼ cup extra-virgin olive oil
1 to 2 tablespoons fresh lemon juice
Freshly ground black pepper
1 6½-ounce can tuna packed in olive oil, drained
2 ounces aged Swiss cheese, cut into julienne strips
2 tablespoons chopped flat-leaf parsley
2 tablespoons capers, drained and chopped

1. Bring a large saucepan of water to a boil. Add the green beans and salt to taste. Cook for 5 minutes or until just tender. Drain and immediately cool the beans under cold running water.
2. In a large bowl whisk together the olive oil, 1 tablespoon lemon juice, and salt and pepper to taste. Stir in the beans and all the remaining ingredients, adding more lemon juice if desired. Serve at room temperature. Do not refrigerate.

GREEN BEAN AND DRIED TOMATO SALAD

Insalata di Fagiolini e Pomodori Secchi

Serves 6

1 pound green beans, trimmed
Salt
½ cup homemade (see page 114) or store-bought dried tomatoes, sliced
¼ cup finely chopped fresh basil
1 garlic clove, peeled and finely chopped
⅓ cup extra-virgin olive oil
3 tablespoons fresh lemon juice
Salt and freshly ground black pepper
2 tablespoons toasted pine nuts

1. Bring a large pot of water to a boil. Add the beans and salt to taste. Cook until the beans are just tender, about 5 minutes. Drain and immediately cool the beans under cold running water.

2. In a large bowl, combine the beans, tomatoes, basil, and garlic. In a small bowl, whisk together the olive oil, lemon juice, and salt and pepper to taste. Pour over the beans and mix well. Sprinkle with the pine nuts. Serve immediately. Do not refrigerate.

TOMATO, ARUGULA, AND RICOTTA SALATA SALAD

Insalata Tricolore

Serves 4

Ricotta salata is a salted and pressed version of fresh ricotta. Combined with tomatoes and arugula, it makes a pretty, three-colored salad.

If ricotta salata is not available, try feta cheese.

1 bunch arugula, washed and dried
2 large ripe tomatoes, thinly sliced
2 thin slices red onion, separated into rings
¼ cup extra-virgin olive oil
Salt and freshly ground black pepper
4 ounces ricotta salata

1. Tear the arugula into bite-size pieces, discarding any tough stems.
2. Arrange the tomatoes on a platter. Top with the arugula and onion rings. Drizzle with the olive oil and sprinkle with salt and pepper to taste.
3. Coarsely grate the ricotta salata. Sprinkle it over the salad. Serve immediately.

SPICY FRESH TOMATO SALAD

Bagnet Rosso

Serves 4 to 6
Makes about 2 cups

This lively mixture is a cross between a salad and a sauce. In Piedmont it is served as a sauce for cold meat. It is also good over hard-cooked eggs or scooped onto crostini.

8 anchovies, finely chopped
2 large ripe tomatoes
2 large garlic cloves, peeled and finely chopped
1 to 2 tablespoons minced seeded hot chili peppers
½ cup chopped red onion
½ cup chopped flat-leaf parsley
1 tablespoon chopped fresh oregano or 1 teaspoon dried
¼ cup extra-virgin olive oil
3 tablespoons red wine vinegar

In a bowl, combine all the ingredients. Let stand for at least 1 hour at room temperature before serving. This can be refrigerated for up to 1 week.

OLIVE AND FENNEL SALAD

Insalata di Olive e Finocchio

Serves 4 to 6

This salad, which is frequently sold in Italian delis, is wonderful with sandwiches, cheese, or a frittata. If you can't find fresh fennel, substitute celery.

8 ounces green Sicilian olives
4 garlic cloves, peeled
2 celery ribs, cut into ¼-inch-thick slices
1 small head fennel, sliced crosswise about ¼ inch thick
¼ teaspoon crushed red pepper, or more to taste
½ teaspoon dried oregano
¼ cup extra-virgin olive oil
2 tablespoons white wine vinegar

1. Place the olives on a cutting board. Crack them open by crushing them lightly with the flat side of a heavy knife. (Removing the pit is optional.) Lightly bruise the garlic cloves in the same way.
2. In a large bowl, combine all of the ingredients. Chill, stirring occasionally, for at least several hours or overnight. Let stand at room temperature for 30 minutes before serving, and remove the garlic cloves. This can be refrigerated for up to 1 week.

Hot Spiced Olives

Olive alla Diavolo

Makes 6 cups

These spicy olives keep indefinitely in the refrigerator. Let them come to room temperature before serving. A bonus here is the marinade, which makes a delicious dip for focaccia.

8 garlic cloves, peeled
1 quart (about 1½ pounds) imported black olives, such as Kalamata or oil-cured
4 1-inch sprigs fresh rosemary or 2 teaspoons dried
4 1-inch strips fresh orange zest
1 teaspoon crushed red pepper
1 teaspoon black peppercorns
About 2 cups extra-virgin olive oil

1. With the side of a heavy knife, lightly crush the garlic. Remove the stem ends.
2. In a 6-cup jar or crock, layer 1 cup of the olives, 2 garlic cloves, a piece each of the rosemary and orange zest, and ¼ teaspoon each of the red pepper and peppercorns. Repeat with the remaining ingredients (except the oil).
3. Add enough olive oil to cover the ingredients completely.
4. Cover the jar and refrigerate for at least 1 week before serving. As the olives are used, add additional oil to the jar as needed so that the olives remain completely submerged. Serve at room temperature. These keep well for up to 1 month.

MARINATED MUSHROOMS

Funghi Sott'Olio

Makes 3 cups

Marinated mushrooms go well with salami and many other antipasti. For spicier mushrooms, add a pinch of crushed red pepper to the marinade. Use the smallest mushrooms you can find. If you must use larger mushrooms, halve or quarter them.

1 cup white wine vinegar
1 teaspoon salt
1¼ pounds (2 10-ounce packages) small
**   mushrooms, cleaned and trimmed**
1 garlic clove, peeled and thinly sliced
1 bay leaf
12 black peppercorns
Extra-virgin olive oil

1. In a large saucepan, combine the vinegar, 2 cups of water, and the salt. Bring to a simmer.
2. Add the mushrooms. Cover and simmer for 6 to 8 minutes, or until tender. Drain. Cool the mushrooms completely.
3. Place the mushrooms, garlic, bay leaf, and peppercorns in a glass jar. Add enough oil to cover the mushrooms. Cover and refrigerate overnight before serving. These can be refrigerated for up to 2 weeks.

TOMATO AND GORGONZOLA SALAD

Insalata di Pomodori e Gorgonzola

Serves 4

Soaking the sliced onion in ice water sweetens it and makes it more digestible.

1 small red onion, peeled and thinly sliced
2 large ripe tomatoes
1 small bunch fresh basil, stems removed and discarded
3 tablespoons extra-virgin olive oil
1 tablespoon red wine vinegar
Salt and freshly ground black pepper
4 ounces imported Italian Gorgonzola, crumbled

1. Place the onion slices in a small bowl. Cover with ice water. Let stand for 30 minutes. Drain and pat dry.

2. Cut the tomatoes into ¼-inch-thick slices. Arrange the tomato and onion slices and basil leaves on a large platter, alternating the ingredients and overlapping them slightly.

3. In a small bowl, whisk together the oil, vinegar, and salt and pepper to taste. Pour the dressing over the vegetables. Sprinkle with the Gorgonzola. Serve immediately.

SHALLOTS IN VINEGAR

Scalogni Sott'Aceto

Makes 6 cups

Paola and Piermario Cavallari are the proprietors of the Grattamacco winery near the Tuscan coast. In addition to growing the grapes for their excellent wines, they maintain a wonderful kitchen garden with all kinds of vegetables, fruits, and herbs. Paola is an excellent cook, and one steamy summer day, she served us a splendid assortment of antipasti which we ate beneath a grape arbor overlooking softly rolling hills that stretched to the sea.

One of the dishes that I most enjoyed was the crunchy pink shallots pickled in wine vinegar. They go very well with cold meats such as salami or ham. Small onions can also be prepared this way.

2 pounds small shallots
2 cups white wine vinegar
2 bay leaves
3 whole cloves
1 3-inch stick cinnamon
3 or 4 sprigs fresh thyme or ½ teaspoon dried
1 tablespoon sugar
1 teaspoon black peppercorns
1 teaspoon salt

1. Bring a large pot of water to a boil. Add the shallots and cook for 1 minute. Drain and rinse under cold running water. Shave off a thin layer from the root ends and slip off the skins.

2. In a large stainless steel or enamel saucepan, bring the vinegar, 1 cup of water, the bay leaves, cloves, cinnamon, thyme, sugar, peppercorns, and salt to a boil. Add the shallots and simmer for 10 minutes. Remove the pan from the heat and let cool.

3. Pour the shallots and the cooking liquid into a covered 6-cup crock or jar. Add water to cover the shallots completely. Cover and refrigerate for at least 1 week before serving. These keep well up to three months.

PICKLED PEPPERS

Peperoni Sott'Aceto

Makes 4 cups

These pickled peppers are great to have on hand during the winter months when fresh peppers may be hard to find. They keep well for up to three months. Serve them, drained and drizzled with olive oil, with strong cheese or salami. They are also good in salads or as an ingredient in many other dishes, such as Potato Salad Artusi (page 98) or Reinforcement Salad (page 92).

4 large red bell peppers, or a combination of red and yellow (about 1½ pounds)
2 large garlic cloves, peeled
1 3-inch sprig fresh oregano or 1 teaspoon dried
1 teaspoon salt
2 cups white wine vinegar

1. Core and seed the peppers and cut them into 1-inch-wide strips. With a paring knife, trim away the white membrane.

2. Pack the peppers into a sterilized quart-size glass jar. Add the garlic, oregano, salt, and vinegar. Add water to cover the peppers completely.

3. Cover and refrigerate for at least 1 week before serving. These keep well for up to 3 months. To serve, drain the peppers and drizzle with olive oil.

BUD'S DRIED TOMATOES

Pomodori Secchi

Makes about 3 cups

This recipe comes from my friend Bud Simon. Home-dried tomatoes are moist and tender and are a great way to preserve a bumper crop. In addition to antipasti, use the dried tomatoes in salads, risotto, pasta, and sauces. They are as good as dried fruits for eating out of hand.

The recipe sounds as if it makes a lot, but the tomatoes will shrink to a fraction of their original size. I usually make as many as my oven can accommodate. Don't be put off by the long cooking time. The tomatoes require very little attention and the oven temperature is so low that it barely heats up the kitchen.

24 large plum tomatoes
Salt
Freshly ground black pepper
About ¼ cup balsamic vinegar

1. Preheat the oven to 250°F. Cut the tomatoes in half lengthwise. With a grapefruit knife, scoop out any white membrane and the seeds and juice.
2. Place the tomato halves cut sides up on a large baking sheet. Sprinkle them lightly with salt and pepper. Spoon ¼ teaspoon balsamic vinegar into each one.
3. Bake the tomatoes for 3 hours or until most of the vinegar is absorbed and the tomatoes are only slightly moist.
4. Turn them and bake for 1 hour more.
5. Turn again and bake for 1 to 2 hours or until the tomatoes are wrinkled and leathery. Let cool. Store the tomatoes in the refrigerator in an airtight container. These will keep well for up to 1 month.

MARINATED DRIED TOMATOES

Pomodori Secchi Marinati

Makes about 4 cups

Use these tomatoes in salads, on crostini, or as a substitute for fresh tomatoes in the winter. The oil is delicious as a dip for focaccia.

1 recipe Bud's Dried Tomatoes (see page 114)
¼ cup fresh basil or 1 teaspoon dried oregano
1 or 2 garlic cloves, peeled and thinly sliced
Extra-virgin olive oil

1. Layer the dried tomatoes, herbs, and garlic in a sterilized 1-quart jar. Add enough oil to cover the tomatoes completely. Cover tightly and refrigerate.
2. Add more oil as needed to keep the tomatoes completely submerged at all times. These keep well for up to 3 months.

EGGS

Le Uova

Eggs, not usually eaten for breakfast in Italy, are more likely to be served as a light lunch or supper or as part of an antipasto, often in the form of a frittata. A frittata is an Italian-style omelet that can include all kinds of vegetables, cheeses, or meats. Usually, frittate are large in size, meant to be cut into wedges to feed several people, but they also can be made small, about as big as a pancake, in which case they are called *frittatine*.

No matter what their size, frittate make wonderful antipasti. They are good hot, cold, or at room temperature. You can make the filling with fresh ingredients or use leftovers.

Hard-cooked eggs are also typical antipasti. They may be sauced, stuffed with tuna, tomatoes, or mayonnaise, or tossed into salads. A pretty and simple presentation is hard-cooked eggs wrapped in prosciutto and fresh basil leaves.

All of the recipes in this book are based on large eggs. Use eggs that are very fresh and never use any that are cracked.

Eggs toughen when cooked too rapidly over high heat, so cook them over a gentle flame. Once cooked, it is difficult to salt frittate (or any scrambled egg dishes) properly, so add the salt to the egg mixture before cooking.

Meglio un uovo

oggi che una

gallina domani.

Better an egg

today than a

chicken tomorrow.

117

ONION AND TOMATO FRITTATA

Frittata di Cipolle e Pomodori

Serves 6

Frittate can be made with all kinds of ingredients. Well-drained canned tomatoes can be used here in place of fresh.

¼ **cup extra-virgin olive oil**
2 **medium onions, peeled and thinly sliced**
1 **large tomato, cored and thinly sliced**
6 **large eggs**
2 **ounces prosciutto, coarsely chopped (about ½ cup)**
¼ **cup freshly grated Parmigiano-Reggiano**
2 **tablespoons chopped fresh basil or flat-leaf parsley**
Salt and freshly ground black pepper

1. In a 10-inch ovenproof skillet, heat 2 tablespoons of the olive oil over medium-low heat. Add the onions and cook, stirring occasionally, until very tender but not browned, about 10 minutes. Stir in the tomato and cook for 10 minutes more. Transfer to a bowl and let cool slightly. Do not clean the pan.

2. In a bowl, beat the eggs until well blended. Stir in the prosciutto, cheese, basil, and salt and pepper to taste. Stir in the onion mixture.

3. In the same skillet, heat the remaining 2 tablespoons oil over medium-low heat. Add the egg mixture. Cook, lifting the edges two or three times to allow the uncooked egg to slide under the cooked portion, until the frittata is set around the edges but still moist in the center, about 10 minutes.

4. Transfer the skillet to the broiler. Cook just until the top of the frittata is set, about 1 minute. Watch carefully so that it does not brown.

5. Invert the frittata onto a serving plate. Serve warm or at room temperature, cut into wedges.

PEPPER AND POTATO FRITTATA

Frittata di Peperoni e Patate

Serves 6

To peel or not to peel depends on the potatoes. If the skins are smooth and relatively unblemished, all that is required is a good scrubbing with a stiff vegetable brush. If the skins are not smooth, the potatoes are better peeled.

¼ cup extra-virgin olive oil
1 large onion, peeled and thinly sliced
2 medium red bell peppers, cored, seeded, and thinly sliced
2 medium all-purpose potatoes, thinly sliced
Salt and freshly ground black pepper
8 large eggs

1. In a 10-inch ovenproof skillet, heat the olive oil over medium-low heat. Add the onion and cook for 5 minutes, stirring occasionally.

2. Add the peppers and potatoes and cook, stirring occasionally, until the potatoes are tender, about 20 minutes. Sprinkle lightly with salt and pepper.

3. Meanwhile, in a bowl, beat the eggs until well blended. Beat in salt and pepper to taste. Add the eggs to the skillet. Cook, lifting the edges two or three times to allow the uncooked egg to slide under the cooked portion, until the frittata is set around the edges but still moist in the center, about 10 minutes.

4. Transfer the skillet to the broiler. Cook just until the top of the frittata is set, about 1 minute. Watch carefully so that the frittata does not brown. Invert the frittata onto a serving plate. Let cool slightly. Serve warm or at room temperature, cut into wedges.

CHICK-PEA FRITTATA

Frittata di Ceci

Serves 6

An unusual frittata flavored with chick-peas, garlic, and parsley. Don't stir the mashed chick-peas in too thoroughly —they should appear as streaks in the egg mixture.

**2 cups drained cooked chick-peas or 1
  19-ounce can chick-peas, rinsed and drained**
8 large eggs
**1 large garlic clove, peeled and very finely
  chopped**
¼ cup chopped flat-leaf parsley
Salt and freshly ground black pepper
2 tablespoons extra-virgin olive oil

1. In a bowl, mash the chick-peas with a fork or a potato masher.
2. Beat the eggs until well blended. Add the garlic, parsley, and salt and pepper to taste. Lightly stir in the chick-peas. The mixture should be somewhat lumpy, not smooth.
3. In a 10-inch ovenproof skillet, heat the oil over medium-low heat. Add the egg mixture. Cook, lifting the edges occasionally to allow the uncooked egg to slide under the cooked portion, until the frittata is set around the edges but still moist in the center, about 10 minutes.
4. Transfer the skillet to the broiler. Cook just until the top of the frittata is set, about 1 minute. Watch carefully so that the frittata does not brown.
5. Invert the frittata onto a serving plate. Let cool slightly. Cut into wedges. Serve warm or at room temperature.

EGG AND TOMATO SALAD

Insalata di Uova e Pomodori

Serves 4

Sliced plum tomatoes are also good in this quick salad.

4 large eggs
1 pint ripe cherry tomatoes, halved
6 scallions, thinly sliced
¼ cup torn fresh basil leaves or chopped flat-leaf parsley
2 tablespoons extra-virgin olive oil
1 tablespoon red wine vinegar
Salt and freshly ground black pepper
Fresh basil leaves

1. Place the eggs in a small saucepan and add warm water to cover. Bring to a simmer over medium-low heat. Simmer gently for 12 minutes. Immediately cool the eggs under cold running water. Drain and peel. Cut the eggs into quarters.
2. In a bowl, combine the eggs, tomatoes, scallions, and basil.
3. Whisk together the olive oil, vinegar, and salt and pepper to taste. Drizzle over the eggs and tomatoes and toss gently. Garnish with the whole basil leaves. Serve immediately.

MINIATURE OMELETS WITH CABBAGE AND LEEKS

Frittatine di Cavolo

Serves 6 to 8

If I had to name the best region in Italy for antipasto, it would be Piedmont. The Piemontese take their antipasti very seriously and instead of serving an assortment on a plate, they are likely to present you with a series of small dishes.

My husband and I had no idea of this, however, when we stopped at the Enoteca del Castello at Costigliole d'Asti for lunch several years ago. The seventeenth-century castle, complete with crenelated tower, houses a collection of locally produced wines, called an *enoteca* or wine library, and a restaurant featuring regional foods.

Our waiter, who could not have been more than fourteen years old, shyly informed us that the menu was set and we only needed to select our wine. Soon our first course appeared—a platter of tender and moist sliced salami and prosciutto, which we enjoyed with the extra-long, crisp *grissini* (breadsticks) for which Piedmont is famous.

When we had finished, we politely laid our forks and knives side by side on our plates to indicate that we were through. The waiter reappeared and, to our surprise, placed the utensils to the sides of the plates as he delivered a tangy, fresh robiola cheese in a green herb sauce.

After this, we again placed the utensils on the plate but again he put them aside to serve *carne cruda*, paper-thin slices of marinated raw veal with shaved white truffles. Roasted peppers in *bagna caôda* followed, then sliced tongue in a garlicky sauce, Gorgonzola-stuffed celery, veal in tuna sauce, and tiny frittatas made with cabbage and leeks. Each time, the fork and knife ritual was repeated.

In all, nine antipasti were served—and we had not expected more than one. Later, we learned that this is not at all unusual in Piedmont, where more elaborate meals have been known to start with as many as thirty antipasti.

Extra-virgin olive oil
3 cups finely shredded cabbage
1 medium leek (white part only), thinly sliced
6 large eggs
½ cup freshly grated Parmigiano-Reggiano
¼ teaspoon salt
⅛ teaspoon freshly ground black pepper

1. In a large heavy skillet, heat 3 tablespoons olive oil over medium-low heat. Stir in the cabbage and leek. Cover the skillet and cook, stirring occasionally, until the cabbage is very tender, about 30 minutes. Let cool.

2. In a large bowl, whisk together the eggs, Parmigiano, salt, and pepper. Stir in the cabbage mixture.

3. Lightly brush a griddle or large skillet with olive oil and heat over medium heat. Stir the egg mixture and scoop by ¼ cupfuls onto the griddle, spacing the omelets about 4 inches apart. Flatten slightly with the back of a spoon. Cook until the edges are set and the omelets begin to brown on the bottom, about 2 minutes. With a pancake turner, flip the omelets and cook on the other side for about 1 minute more. Transfer the omelets to a plate. Keep warm, if desired, in a low oven.

4. Cook the remainder of the omelet mixture in the same way, brushing the griddle with oil as needed. Serve hot, warm, or cold.

EGGS WITH BASIL AND PROSCIUTTO

Uova con Prosciutto e Basilico

Serves 4

Tender, perfectly cooked eggs are lovely with prosciutto, olive oil, and basil.

4 large eggs
Freshly ground black pepper
12 small fresh basil leaves
8 thin slices prosciutto (about 2 ounces)
2 tablespoons extra-virgin olive oil

1. Place the eggs in a small saucepan and add warm water to cover. Bring to a simmer over medium-low heat. Cook for 12 minutes. Immediately cool the eggs under cold running water. Drain and peel.

2. Cut the eggs in half lengthwise. Sprinkle the cut sides with pepper. Place a basil leaf on each. Fold the prosciutto slices in half lengthwise. Wrap 1 slice of prosciutto around the center of each egg half. Place the eggs on a plate and drizzle with the olive oil. Garnish with the remaining basil. Serve immediately.

EGGS STUFFED WITH CAPERS

Uova Ripiene di Capperi

Serves 4 to 8

4 large eggs
2 tablespoons unsalted butter, at room temperature
1 tablespoon finely chopped drained capers
2 teaspoons anchovy paste
Salt and freshly ground black pepper
8 whole capers

1. Place the eggs in a small saucepan and add warm water to cover. Bring to a simmer over medium-low heat. Cook for 12 minutes. Immediately cool the eggs under cold running water. Drain and peel.

2. Cut the eggs in half lengthwise and scoop the yolks into a bowl. Mash the yolks and blend in the butter. Stir in the chopped capers, anchovy paste, and salt and pepper to taste. Stuff the whites with this mixture, mounding it slightly. Garnish each half with a caper. Serve immediately.

TUNA-STUFFED EGGS

Uova Ripiene di Tonno

Serves 4

4 large eggs
Radicchio or red-leaf lettuce leaves
¼ cup drained canned oil-packed tuna
3 tablespoons softened butter
1 tablespoon freshly grated Parmigiano-Reggiano
Small pinch of grated nutmeg
1 tablespoon finely chopped flat-leaf parsley

1. Place the eggs in a small saucepan with warm water to cover. Bring to a simmer over medium-low heat. Cook for 12 minutes. Immediately cool the eggs under cold running water.

2. Peel the eggs and cut them in half lengthwise. Place the yolks in a medium bowl. Arrange the whites on a plate lined with the lettuce leaves.

3. Add the tuna to the egg yolks and mash with a wooden spoon. Beat in the butter, cheese, and nutmeg. Stir in the parsley.

4. Spoon the mixture into the egg whites. Cover and chill for 1 hour before serving.

EGGS IN TUNA SAUCE

Uova in Salsa di Tonno

Serves 6

This lovely sauce is traditionally served over poached veal as an antipasto or main course in the summer. I also like it as a topping for crostini, as a dip for raw endive, or as a sauce for hard-cooked eggs.

6 large eggs
1 6½-ounce can tuna packed in olive oil
4 anchovy fillets
½ cup mayonnaise, preferably homemade (see page 241)
2 tablespoons capers, drained
1 small garlic clove, peeled
1½ to 2 tablespoons fresh lemon juice
Chopped flat-leaf parsley

1. Place the eggs in a small saucepan with warm water to cover. Bring to a simmer over medium-low heat. Cook for 12 minutes. Immediately cool the eggs under cold running water.
2. In a a food processor or blender, combine the tuna with its oil, anchovies, mayonnaise, capers, and garlic. Process until smooth, about 3 minutes, stopping to scrape the mixture down as necessary. Add lemon juice to taste.
3. Peel the eggs and cut them in half lengthwise. Place the eggs cut sides down in a serving dish and spoon on the sauce. Sprinkle with the parsley. Serve immediately.

EGGS IN A RED SHIRT

Uova in Camicia Rossa

Serves 6

When these cooled poached eggs, topped with fresh, herbed tomatoes, are cut open, the still-soft yolks blend with the tomatoes to form a rich sauce. Nice for an antipasto brunch or buffet.

2 medium tomatoes, peeled, seeded, and chopped
2 tablespoons extra-virgin olive oil
2 tablespoons chopped fresh basil or flat-leaf parsley
Pinch of dried oregano
Salt and freshly ground black pepper
6 large eggs
¼ cup white wine vinegar

1. In a shallow serving dish, combine the tomatoes, oil, basil, oregano, and salt and pepper to taste. Set aside.

2. In a large deep skillet, bring 2 quarts of water to a simmer. Add the vinegar. Crack the eggs one at a time and slide them into the water, keeping them several inches apart. Cover and cook over low heat for 4 minutes. Remove the eggs with a slotted spoon and gently blot them dry with paper towels. (If the eggs are not very fresh, the white will spread out from the yolk as they cook. If necessary, trim away some of the white from the cooked eggs to give them a neat appearance.)

3. Place the eggs in the tomato mixture, spooning some of the tomatoes over the eggs. Serve at room temperature.

CHEESE

Il Formaggio

~~~~~~

Italians make hundreds of cheeses from cow's, sheep's, and goat's milk. Many are exported and are well worth seeking out. Just be sure when buying any of these cheeses that they are in good condition. Too often, especially imported fresh cheese like mozzarella or delicate cheese like Gorgonzola suffer from their long journey. Look at, sniff, and taste the cheese before you commit yourself to purchasing it. If the edges are browned and cracked or if the cheese smells of ammonia, don't buy it. Also, avoid precut, prepackaged cheeses. It is hard to judge their age and quality and they are likely to have picked up stale odors from the foods around them.

I have made suggestions for alternative cheeses wherever possible in these recipes. The result may not be authentic, but it will surely taste better than it would using a cheese in poor condition.

Cheese tastes best and has a better texture when it is at room temperature. Remove cheese from the refrigerator at least an hour before serving.

Italians do not serve a cheese assortment as an antipasto because they feel that a variety of cheeses would be too rich before a meal. Cheeses are more likely served after the main course instead of, or before, dessert. One or two cheeses at most are served as part of an antipasto—perhaps a perfectly fresh mozzarella or a marinated soft cheese like caprino or robiola.

Vino che frizzi,

pane che canti,

e formaggio che

pizzichi.

~~~~~~~~~~~~~~~~

Wine that bubbles,

bread that sings,

and cheese that

tingles.

Mozzarella with Parsley and Garlic

Mozzarella con Prezzemolo e Aglio

Serves 6 to 8

The zesty sauce of parsley and garlic improves as it stands and makes a lively contrast to the mildness of the mozzarella.

¼ cup extra-virgin olive oil
2 tablespoons finely chopped flat-leaf parsley
1 garlic clove, peeled and finely chopped
Pinch of crushed red pepper
Salt and freshly ground black pepper
1 pound mozzarella, fresh if possible

1. In a bowl, combine the olive oil, parsley, garlic, red pepper, salt to taste, and a generous pinch of pepper. Let stand at room temperature for at least 1 hour.

2. Cut the mozzarella into ¼-inch-thick slices. Arrange them overlapping on a plate. Just before serving, stir the sauce and spoon it over the cheese.

Marinated Mozzarella "Cherries"

Ciliegine Marinate

Serves 6

Ciliegine ("little cherries") are little balls of fresh mozzarella. Creamy and chewy, they are a perfect size for antipasti and are delicious plain or with a dressing. There is only one problem—they are hard to find. However, the Polly-O Dairy Company has introduced a line of high-quality fresh mozzarella packed in water in various shapes and sizes that can be found in many supermarkets in the Northeast. If ciliegine are not available, cut a larger piece of mozzarella into bite-size chunks.

½ cup homemade (see page 114) or store-bought dried tomatoes, cut into thin strips (if the tomatoes are packed in oil, drain them, reserving the oil)

2 tablespoons chopped fresh flat-leaf basil or parsley

Pinch of dried oregano

3 tablespoons extra-virgin olive oil (or the marinating oil from the tomatoes)

Freshly ground black pepper

1 9-ounce package ciliegine di mozzarella or 8 ounces fresh mozzarella cut into ¾-inch chunks

1. In a bowl, combine the tomatoes, basil, oregano, oil, and pepper to taste.

2. If using ciliegine packed in water, drain them and blot dry with paper towels. Add the cheese to the tomato mixture and stir gently. Cover and let stand at room temperature for at least 1 hour before serving.

MARINATED GOAT CHEESE

Caprino Marinato

Serves 4 to 6

A warm, golden, late fall day in Asti turned into a cold, chilly night as the densest fog I have ever experienced swept through the narrow streets of the darkened town. It seemed foolhardy to drive anywhere over the unfamiliar country roads, so we decided to stay in town. But how to pass the long evening? As we stumbled through the nearly impenetrable fog, a figure stepped out of the swirling mist and thrust a paper into our hands. It was a handbill advertising a grappa convention in town that night. What more could we have asked for?

Grappa is an Italian form of brandy that is distilled from the skins, seeds, and stems of grapes that have been pressed to make wine. A clear white to amber liquid, it is made in many different styles, all of them quite potent. My husband, a grappa aficionado, was delighted with the idea of a grappa convention. Even I, who generally find grappa too strong to drink, found the thought of a warming glass of grappa appealing on that bone-chilling night.

A large, cheerful crowd filled the room where the conference was being held. We looked at exhibits of grappa-making equipment and grappa-making techniques, then passed into a second room where the actual tastings were held. It was there I learned that grappa can also be an excellent ingredient for a variety of creations. We tasted a pumpkin-and-apple cake flavored with grappa, chocolates filled with grappa, grappa cocktails, and even a snail soup with grappa. All were good, but the real standout was the goat cheese marinated with a dash of grappa.

Caprino, from *capra*, meaning "goat," is the Italian name for goat cheese. If you can't find caprino, any mild fresh goat cheese will do, and you can substitute vodka for the grappa if necessary.

1 6-ounce log or round caprino or other mild
   fresh goat cheese
2 tablespoons chopped fresh parsley
1 small garlic clove, peeled and crushed
⅛ teaspoon ground red pepper
2 tablespoons extra-virgin olive oil
1 tablespoon grappa or vodka
Toasted sliced Italian bread

1. Place the cheese in a small container. In a bowl, combine the remaining ingredients except the bread and pour over the cheese. Cover and refrigerate for at least 24 hours.
2. Serve at room temperature with toasted Italian bread. This keeps well for up to 3 days.

TALEGGIO WITH OLIVE OIL

Taleggio all'Olio

Serves 6 to 8

This is so simple it almost does not need a recipe. Many other semisoft cheeses may be served this way, such as fresh mozzarella, mild Pecorino, or fresh caprino (goat cheese). Just be sure to use your best olive oil.

8 ounces Taleggio or other semisoft cheese, cut
   into ¼-inch-thick slices, at room temperature
Extra-virgin olive oil
Coarsely ground black pepper

Arrange the cheese slices overlapping slightly on a plate. Drizzle lightly with olive oil. Sprinkle generously with pepper. Serve immediately.

ELECTRIC CHEESE

Formaggio Elettrico

Serves 4 to 6

Italians—especially those from the North, where this recipe originates—rarely eat hot spicy foods, so this is called electric cheese because it give you a bit of a shock when you taste it. You can adjust the hotness to your own taste.

Robiola cheese is typically used. *Robiola* is the name of a whole family of soft white cheeses from Piedmont, which can be made from cow's, sheep's and/or goat's milk.

6 ounces fresh robiola or mild fresh goat cheese
Freshly ground black pepper
¼ cup extra-virgin olive oil
1 tablespoon tomato puree or very finely chopped fresh tomato
1 to 2 teaspoons finely minced fresh hot chili pepper
1 teaspoon white wine vinegar
Pinch of salt
Toasted Italian bread

1. Place the cheese in a small container. Sprinkle generously with pepper.
2. In a bowl, whisk together the remaining ingredients except the bread and pour over the cheese. Cover and refrigerate overnight or up to 3 days before serving. Serve with slices of toasted Italian bread.

PIEMONTESE GREEN GARLIC CHEESE

Agliata Verde del Piemonte

Serves 6

This cheese spread is usually served as a companion to Cipollata Rossa (page 140).

10 tender celery leaves
10 fresh basil leaves
½ cup packed flat-leaf parsley leaves
2 large garlic cloves, peeled
Freshly ground black pepper
6-ounces robiola or mild fresh goat cheese
Fresh lemon juice
Salt
Toasted Italian bread

1. In a food processor or blender, combine the celery leaves, basil, parsley, and garlic. Finely chop. Add pepper to taste and process to blend.
2. Break the cheese into chunks. Add it to the herb mixture and process until smooth. Season to taste with lemon juice and salt.
3. Pack the mixture into a small container. Cover and refrigerate overnight or up to 3 days before serving. Serve with slices of toasted Italian bread.

MELTED FONTINA CHEESE

Fonduta

Serves 4

Fonduta is a rich and creamy blend of melted fontina cheese, eggs, and milk. In Piedmont, in Northern Italy, fonduta is usually served over toast as an antipasto. It may also be used as a sauce for risotto or as a filling for puff pastry tartlets.

The sauve richness of fonduta is also a perfect backdrop for one of Piedmont's most famous products, the white truffle. In Piedmont, truffles can be found growing amid the roots of oak trees, and specially trained dogs are employed to sniff out their location. The truffles are highly prized, even more so than the black variety.

It is rare to find fresh truffles here and if you do find them, they may not be at their best. A fresh truffle should have a strong, earthy aroma and feel firm when pressed. Canned truffles are not very good and are not worth the expense.

Even if you don't have a truffle, the fonduta will be delicious. Try to find authentic Italian fontina. It is a lovely, mild, semisoft cheese with a natural rind and subtle flavor reminiscent of truffles. It makes a fine dessert cheese too.

8 ounces Italian fontina
1 cup whole milk
3 tablespoons unsalted butter
3 egg yolks
8 thin slices whole wheat Italian bread, toasted
1 or 2 large garlic cloves, peeled
Thin shavings of white truffle, optional

1. Remove the rind from the cheese. Cut the cheese into small dice. Place the cheese in a bowl and add the milk. Cover with plastic wrap and refrigerate overnight.

2. In the top of a double boiler set over simmering water, melt the butter. Drain half the milk from the cheese into a small bowl and set aside. Pour the remaining cheese mixture into the double boiler with the butter. Cook, stirring frequently with a wooden spoon, until the cheese is melted.

3. Beat the egg yolks with the reserved milk and stir the mixture into the cheese. Cook, stirring frequently, until smooth and slightly thickened, about 5 minutes. Remove from the heat.

4. Rub the bread slices with the garlic. Place 2 slices on each plate. Pour the fonduta over the bread. Garnish with the white truffle slices, if using.

GOLDEN CHEESE AND PROSCIUTTO SANDWICHES

Pandorato

Serves 4

These sandwiches can be halved or quartered. Serve them before dinner with drinks or wine.

4 thin slices prosciutto

4 thin slices Italian fontina, asiago fresco, or Bel Paese

8 slices chewy peasant-style bread (about 3- × 2- × ⅓-inch)

2 tablespoons unsalted butter

2 tablespoons extra-virgin olive oil

1. Layer the prosciutto and cheese on 4 slices of the bread. Cover with the remaining bread.

2. In a large skillet, heat the butter with the olive oil over medium-low heat until foaming. Add the sandwiches and cook, turning once, until the cheese is melted and the bread is golden, about 10 minutes.

3. Cut into halves or quarters and serve hot.

FRIED MOZZARELLA STICKS

Bastoncini di Mozzarella Fritti

Makes about 20 sticks

For a crisp, crunchy crust and a melting center, it is essential to coat the cheese thoroughly with the flour, eggs, and bread crumbs so that the cheese does not seep through as it melts. Also, be sure the oil is hot enough to brown the coating quickly.

8 ounces chilled whole-milk mozzarella
3 cups fine dry bread crumbs
Salt and freshly ground black pepper
½ cup all-purpose flour
3 large eggs
Vegetable oil for frying

1. Cut the mozzarella into 3- × ½- × ½-inch sticks.
2. On a piece of wax paper, combine the bread crumbs and salt and pepper to taste. Spread the flour on a separate piece of wax paper. In a shallow bowl, beat the eggs.
3. Roll the cheese sticks one at a time in the flour. Dip them in the beaten eggs, turning them several times to coat thoroughly—be sure to coat the ends.
4. Roll the cheese in the bread crumbs, again in the eggs, and then again in the bread crumbs. Let dry on a wire rack for 15 to 30 minutes.
5. Pour about ½ inch of oil into a large heavy skillet. Heat the oil over medium heat until the temperature reaches 375°F on a deep-frying thermometer.
6. Add the cheese sticks to the oil a few at a time so that they are not crowded. Fry until golden brown, turning once, about 2 minutes. Drain on paper towels. Repeat with the remaining cheese sticks. Serve immediately.

GRILLED MOZZARELLA AND DRIED TOMATO SKEWERS

Spiedini di Mozzarella e Pomodori alla Griglia

Serves 8

Another variation on the mozzarella and tomato theme. Skewers of barely melted mozzarella and dried tomatoes are an easy antipasto for a barbecue.

24 pieces marinated dried tomatoes (either homemade, see page 115, or store-bought), with their oil
1 pound mozzarella, cut into 1-inch cubes, or 1 pound fresh ciliegine (see page 131)
16 fresh basil leaves

1. Preheat a grill or broiler. Lightly brush the grill rack or broiler pan with oil.
2. On each of 8 short skewers, thread 3 pieces of tomato, 2 cubes of mozzarella, and 2 basil leaves, alternating the ingredients and beginning and ending with a piece of tomato. Brush the cheese with some of the marinade from the tomatoes.
3. Grill or broil the skewers just until the cheese begins to melt, turning once. Serve immediately.

RED PEPPER AND ONION CHEESE

Cipollata Rossa

Serves 6 to 8

Serve this red cheese with green Agliata Verde (page 135) for an appealing combination of contrasting colors on an antipasto table.

Don't try to prepare this in the food processor or it will become too runny. It should have a spreadable consistency.

6 ounces robiola or mild fresh goat cheese
½ cup minced red bell pepper
2 tablespoons minced onion
1 teaspoon chopped fresh hot red chili pepper or
¼ teaspoon ground red pepper
½ teaspoon sweet paprika
1 tablespoon fresh lemon juice
1 tablespoon extra-virgin olive oil
Toasted Italian bread

1. In a bowl, combine the cheese, bell pepper, and onion and beat with a wooden spoon until well blended.
2. Beat in the chili pepper, paprika, lemon juice, and olive oil until well blended.
3. Pack the mixture into a small bowl and cover tightly. Refrigerate overnight or up to 3 days before serving. Serve at room temperature with slices of toasted Italian bread.

PARMESAN WITH DATES

Parmigiano coi Datteri

Serves 8

One would never guess that a rather nondescript little town like Labico, south of Rome, would be the home of a culinary gem. On a blistering hot summer day we passed the restaurant La Vecchia Osteria four times before we finally found the entrance.

Inside, it was cool and dark, a pleasant contrast to the streets outside. While we pondered the menu, we were served this lovely antipasto with glasses of well-chilled Ca del Bosco spumante. The combination of sweet dates, nutty-tasting cheese, and sparkling wine was sensational.

This is great as an impromptu antipasto if you have the ingredients on hand. I find that the dates in my local health food store are moister and more tender than the supermarket variety. Use a young, not too dry Parmigiano.

8 ounces pitted dates
4 ounces Parmigiano-Reggiano, at room
temperature

1. Split the dates in half lengthwise. Open each date like a book.
2. With a small knife, cut or break the Parmigiano into thin pieces roughly the same length as the dates. Press a piece of cheese into each date and serve.

RICOTTA FRITTERS

Crochette di Ricotta

Makes about 12 fritters
Serves 4 to 6

These delicious little fritters from Emilia-Romagna can also be served as a dessert. Substitute sugar to taste for the Parmigiano and add a bit of grated lemon zest. Sprinkle the hot sweet fritters with additional sugar. Freshly made ricotta is great if you can find it.

1 cup ricotta
2 large eggs
¼ cup freshly grated Parmigiano-Reggiano
About 3 tablespoons all-purpose flour
Freshly ground black pepper
1 cup dry bread crumbs
Vegetable oil for frying

1. Place the ricotta in a strainer set over a bowl. With a rubber spatula, press the ricotta through the strainer. Add 1 of the eggs, the Parmigiano, 3 tablespoons flour, and pepper to taste. Beat until well blended. The mixture should be thick enough to hold a soft shape. If it is not, add a teaspoon or more flour.
2. In a shallow bowl, beat the remaining egg. Spread the bread crumbs on a piece of wax paper.
3. Shape the cheese mixture into 1-inch balls. Roll them in the beaten egg and then in the bread crumbs, patting gently to make the crumbs adhere. Let dry for 15 to 30 minutes on a wire rack.
4. Pour enough oil to come to a depth of 2 inches into a deep fryer or heavy saucepan. Heat the oil over medium heat until the temperature measures 375°F on a deep-frying thermometer.
5. Slip the fritters, a few at a time, into the hot oil. Fry, turning, until golden brown on all sides, about 4 minutes. Remove with a slotted spoon and drain on paper towels. Keep warm in a low oven while frying the remainder of the fritters.

CROSTINI AND BRUSCHETTA

Non c'è

cibo da re

più saporito

del pane.

No food

eaten by a king

is tastier

than bread.

While *crostini* literally means "toast" in Italian, the term also refers to slices of toast spread with an endless choice of savory toppings. Crostini in one form or another are typical antipasti throughout Italy, especially in Tuscany, where chicken liver–topped crostini are served with assorted salumi as the classic starter to many rustic meals.

The quality of bread used to make crostini is very important. It should be firm and crusty around the edges while the middle is chewy, yet soft enough to soak up any juices that might leak from the topping without falling apart. Pane Toscano (page 158) is ideal for crostini, but a good Italian or French loaf or a peasant-style bread can be used.

Don't assemble the crostini too far in advance or the bread may become soggy. Though Italians would never do this, I sometimes serve the bread and topping separately and let everyone help themselves.

Almost any topping is suitable for crostini. In addition to the recipes in this chapter, other possibilities include Peperonata (page 41), Bagnet Rosso (page 107), and Caponata (page 94).

Bruschetta (pronounced bruce-ketta), is another type of crostini, but thicker bread is toasted on a grill, preferably over a wood fire, and spread with a very light topping, usually just fresh garlic and olive oil. In Umbria and sometimes in Tuscany, it is called *fettunta*, meaning "oiled slice."

Bruschetta is the original garlic bread and no antipasto could be more delicious, or simple, to make. Failing the wood fire, you can make bruschetta on a barbecue, on a stovetop griddle, or in the broiler. Since there are so few ingredients in bruschetta, each one must be at its best: coarse peasant bread, fruity green olive oil, and fresh garlic. If you are using unsalted Tuscan-style bread, you might want to sprinkle the toast with coarse salt before serving.

Bruschetta goes with all kinds of antipasti or just serve it on its own with a hunk of flavorful cheese, such as Parmigiano or Grana Padano.

OLIVE CROSTINI

Crostini di Olive

Makes 8 crostini

½ cup pitted imported black olives, such as
    Kalamata
3 anchovy fillets
1 tablespoon drained capers
1 garlic clove, peeled
2 tablespoons extra-virgin olive oil
8 slices Crostini (see at right)

In the bowl of a food processor, finely chop the olives, anchovies, capers, and garlic. Place in a bowl and stir in the olive oil. Spread on the toasted bread. Serve immediately.

Crostini di Olive e Mozzarella Assemble Olive Crostini as directed. Top each with a slice of fresh mozzarella. Preheat the oven to 400°F, and bake for 5 minutes, or until the cheese is slightly melted. Serve hot.

TOASTING CROSTINI

To toast the bread for crostini, bake ½-inch-thick slices of Pane Toscano (see page 158) or other chewy, peasant-style bread in a preheated 400°F oven for 15 minutes, or until lightly browned, turning once.

FIG CROSTINI

Crostini di Ficchi

Makes 4 crostini

My husband adores figs and just can't resist the combination of the sweet, honeylike fruits with prosciutto. Needless to say, he was thrilled when these crostini arrived with his plate of prosciutto at Da Delfina, a picturesque country restaurant in the hilltop town of Artimino, just outside of Florence.

To peel or not to peel figs before serving is not an option in Tuscany—figs are always peeled. In fact, the skin of a fig is considered potentially lethal, as it may stick in your throat. An old Tuscan saying admonishes darkly, "Give the skin of the fig to your enemy, and the skin of the peach to your friends."

2 medium ripe figs (black or green)
Honey, optional
4 slices Crostini (see page 145)

1. Peel the figs and mash them with a fork. Add a drop or two (no more) of honey, if necessary, to sweeten them.
2. Spread the figs on the bread. Serve as an accompaniment to thin slices of prosciutto or salami.

DRIED TOMATO CROSTINI

Crostini di Pomodori Secchi

Makes 12 crostini

The intense flavor of dried tomatoes is especially appreciated when ripe tomatoes are out of season.

1 cup homemade (see page 114) or store-bought dried tomatoes (if the tomatoes are packed in oil, drain them, reserving the oil)
1 small garlic clove, peeled
Pinch of dried oregano
6 tablespoons extra-virgin olive oil (or the marinating oil from the tomatoes)
12 slices ½-inch-thick Pane Toscano (see page 158) or chewy peasant-style bread
12 thin slices smoked or fresh mozzarella
12 small fresh basil or flat-leaf parsley leaves

1. Preheat the oven to 400°F.
2. Very finely chop the tomatoes and garlic. Transfer to a small bowl and stir in the oregano and 2 tablespoons of the oil.
3. Arrange the bread slices on a baking sheet. Bake, turning the slices once, for 15 to 20 minutes, or until lightly browned on both sides. Remove the pan from the oven but leave the oven on. Brush the bread on one side with the remaining 4 tablespoons olive oil.
4. Spread the tomato mixture on the bread. Top with the mozzarella slices. Bake for 5 minutes, or until the mozzarella is slightly melted. Garnish with the basil leaves. Serve hot.

CHICKEN LIVER CROSTINI

Crostini di Fegatini di Pollo

Makes 12 crostini

Every Tuscan cook has his or her own version of these crostini. I like this one with its tangy taste of capers and anchovies.

2 tablespoons extra-virgin olive oil
8 ounces chicken livers, trimmed and coarsely
  chopped
¼ cup finely chopped flat-leaf parsley
4 fresh sage leaves, finely chopped
¼ cup drained capers, chopped
3 anchovy fillets, finely chopped
1 tablespoon red wine vinegar
Salt and freshly ground black pepper
12 slices Crostini (see page 145)

1. In a medium skillet, heat the oil over medium heat. Add the livers, parsley, sage, and capers. Cook, stirring frequently, for 10 minutes, or just until the livers lose their pink color.
2. Stir in the anchovies, vinegar, and salt and pepper to taste. Spread on the warm toast. Serve immediately.

BEAN AND GREENS CROSTINI

Crostini alla Pugliese

Makes 12 crostini

These are hearty "knife-and-fork" crostini, not the kind you should attempt to eat out of hand. They are a good starter for a country-style meal of grilled sausages or a pork roast, or as a meatless supper on their own.

¼ cup extra-virgin olive oil
2 large garlic cloves, peeled and finely chopped
1 pound broccoli rabe or spinach, washed and trimmed
½ teaspoon salt
¼ teaspoon crushed red pepper
2½ cups drained cooked cannellini beans (see page 74) or 1 19-ounce can cannellini beans, rinsed and drained
½ teaspoon dried sage, crumbled
Freshly ground black pepper
12 slices Crostini (see page 145)

1. In a large saucepan, heat 2 tablespoons of the olive oil over medium heat. Add half the garlic and sauté for 30 seconds. Add the greens, salt, and red pepper. Cover and cook until tender, about 10 minutes for broccoli rabe or 5 minutes for spinach. Remove from the heat.

2. Meanwhile, in a medium saucepan, heat the remaining 2 tablespoons olive oil over medium heat. Add the remaining garlic and sauté for 30 seconds. Stir in the beans, 2 tablespoons of water, the sage, and black pepper to taste. Reduce the heat to low. Cover and cook for 10 minutes. Remove from the heat. Coarsely mash the beans with a wooden spoon.

3. Spread the toasted bread slices with the beans. Top with the greens and serve immediately.

MUSHROOM AND FONTINA CROSTINI

Crostini ai Funghi e Fontina

Makes 8 crostini

A "knife-and-fork" crostino from the Trattoria Vecchia Roma in Rome's Piazza Campitelli.

2 tablespoons unsalted butter
¼ cup extra-virgin olive oil
1 garlic clove, peeled and finely chopped
12 ounces thinly sliced white mushrooms
½ teaspoon salt
¼ teaspoon dried rosemary, crumbled
⅛ teaspoon dried marjoram
Freshly ground black pepper
8 slices ½-inch-thick Pane Toscano (see page 158) or chewy peasant-style bread
6 ounces Italian fontina or Bel Paese, thinly sliced

1. Preheat the broiler.
2. In a large skillet, heat the butter and 2 tablespoons of the olive oil over medium heat. Add the garlic and cook, stirring, for 30 seconds. Stir in the mushrooms, salt, rosemary, marjoram, and pepper to taste. Cook, stirring frequently, until the mushrooms are lightly browned, about 10 minutes.
3. Meanwhile, arrange the bread on a baking sheet. Toast under the broiler, turning once, until lightly browned on both sides. Brush with the remaining 2 tablespoons olive oil. Leave the broiler on.
4. Spoon the mushrooms and pan juices over the toasted bread. Top with the fontina. Broil for 2 minutes or until the cheese begins to melt. Serve immediately.

WILD MUSHROOM CROSTINI

Crostini ai Funghi Porcini

Makes 12 crostini

1 ounce dried porcini mushrooms
1½ cups warm water
8 tablespoons (1 stick) unsalted butter
1 medium onion, peeled and chopped
8 ounces white mushrooms, sliced
3 medium carrots, peeled and grated
1 bay leaf
1 cup dry white wine
Salt and freshly ground black pepper
1½ tablespoons capers, drained and chopped
12 slices Crostini (see page 145)
Extra-virgin olive oil

1. In a bowl, soak the porcini in the water for 30 minutes. Lift the mushrooms from the liquid and set aside. Strain the liquid through a double thickness of dampened cheesecloth or paper towels. Set aside. Wash the mushrooms well under cool running water, looking them over carefully to remove all traces of sand. Finely chop.

2. In a large skillet, melt the butter over medium heat. Add the onion and cook, stirring frequently, until tender, about 5 minutes.

3. Add the porcini, white mushrooms, carrots, bay leaf, wine, mushroom soaking liquid, and salt and pepper to taste. Cook, stirring occasionally, for 45 minutes or until most of the liquid has evaporated.

4. Stir in the capers. Discard the bay leaf.

5. Spread the mixture on the crostini. Drizzle each with a few drops of oil. Serve warm.

Crostini ai Funghi con Prosciutto Prepare the crostini as directed, omitting the olive oil. Top each with a thin slice of prosciutto.

GARLIC TOAST

Bruschetta

Makes 8 bruschetta

8 slices ¾-inch-thick Pane Toscano (see page
   158) or other chewy peasant-style bread
3 large garlic cloves, peeled
Extra-virgin olive oil
Coarse salt, optional

1. Preheat a barbecue grill, griddle, or broiler.
2. Toast the bread until lightly browned on both sides, turning once. Immediately rub one side of each slice with the garlic. Drizzle generously with olive oil. Sprinkle with salt, if desired. Serve immediately.

FRESH TOMATO TOAST

Bruschetta con Pomodori

Makes 12 bruschetta

Fresh garlic toast topped with a chopped tomato salad makes a perfect antipasto for a cookout. The bread soaks up all of the delicious juices, so not a drop is wasted.

2 medium ripe tomatoes, cored and chopped
¼ cup extra-virgin olive oil
½ teaspoon coarse salt
¼ teaspoon freshly ground black pepper
12 fresh basil leaves
12 slices ¾-inch-thick Pane Toscano (see page
   158) or chewy peasant-style bread
3 large garlic cloves, peeled

1. In a medium bowl, combine the tomatoes, olive oil, salt, and pepper. Tear the basil leaves into small pieces and stir in. Let the mixture stand at room temperature for 30 minutes.

2. Preheat the broiler or grill.

3. Toast the bread until lightly browned on both sides, turning once. Immediately rub one side of each slice with the garlic cloves. Spoon the tomato mixture onto the toast and serve immediately.

Bruschetta con Pomodori e Arugula Prepare the bruschetta as indicated. Top each piece with coarsely chopped arugula.

PARMESAN TOAST

Bruschetta con Parmigiano

Makes 8 bruschetta

8 slices ¾-inch-thick Pane Toscano (see page 158) or chewy peasant-style bread
2 garlic cloves, peeled
⅓ cup extra-virgin olive oil
½ cup freshly grated Parmigiano-Reggiano
Freshly ground black pepper

1. Preheat the broiler.

2. Toast the bread until lightly browned on both sides, turning once. Leave the broiler on.

3. Rub one side of each slice with the garlic and brush with the olive oil. Sprinkle with the Parmigiano and pepper.

4. Broil for 1 minute or until the cheese melts. Serve immediately.

SKEWERED MOZZARELLA SANDWICHES WITH ANCHOVY SAUCE

Spiedini alla Romana

Makes 4 sandwiches

These are a form of crostini, but instead of toasting the bread first, then putting on a topping, the bread and cheese are threaded on skewers and toasted together. Then a little bit of anchovy sauce is used to moisten the whole thing.

My mother used to make me sandwiches similar to this when I was a child. She would layer the cheese between two slices of bread, coat the sandwiches with beaten egg, and then sauté them until golden. She would prepare the anchovy sauce in the same skillet. Pretty sophisticated fare for a child, you say? Well, I never was one for peanut butter and jelly.

12 slices ½-inch-thick Italian or French bread
8 ounces fresh mozzarella, cut into ¼-inch-thick slices
4 tablespoons unsalted butter
1 tablespoon extra-virgin olive oil
1 garlic clove, peeled and finely chopped
6 anchovy fillets
Freshly ground black pepper

1. Preheat the oven to 450°. Brush a large baking sheet with oil.

2. On each of 4 short skewers, thread 3 slices of the bread and 2 of mozzarella, alternating the slices and beginning and ending with bread. Place on the prepared baking sheet. Bake for 20 minutes or until the bread is toasted and the cheese is partially melted.

3. Meanwhile, in a small saucepan, melt the butter with the olive oil and garlic over medium heat. Add the anchovies and pepper to taste and stir until the anchovies dissolve.

4. Transfer the spiedini to warm serving plates, sliding them off the skewers. Pour the anchovy sauce over the sandwiches and serve immediately.

HERBED TOAST

Bruschetta alle Erbe

Makes 8 bruschetta

If you have no fresh herbs, use dried in whichever combination you prefer. Let them steep for a while in the oil to soften them and release their aromas.

⅓ cup extra-virgin olive oil
1 tablespoon chopped flat-leaf parsley
1 tablespoon chopped fresh basil
Pinch of dried marjoram
Freshly ground black pepper
8 slices ¾-inch-thick Pane Toscano (see page 158) or chewy peasant-style bread
2 large garlic cloves, peeled

1. In a small bowl, combine the oil, herbs, and pepper to taste.
2. Preheat the grill or broiler.
3. Toast the bread until lightly browned on both sides, turning once. Immediately rub one side of each slice with the garlic. Brush with the herb mixture. Serve immediately.

TOMATO TOAST

Frega

Makes 4 crostini

Signora Paola Cavallari of the Grattamacco winery in Tuscany told me that these toasts are called *frega*, meaning "rub," by the farmers who eat them for their afternoon snack or *merenda*.

They are a good way to use up slightly overripe tomatoes.

1 large ripe tomato
4 slices ½-inch-thick Pane Toscano (see page 158) or chewy peasant-style bread
2 large garlic cloves, peeled
Extra-virgin olive oil
Salt and freshly ground black pepper

1. Preheat the broiler or grill.
2. With a sharp knife, remove a patch of skin from the tomato.
3. Toast the bread until lightly browned on both sides, turning once. Immediately rub one side of each slice with the garlic cloves. Rub the peeled side of the tomato over the garlic-rubbed side of the bread, squeezing gently until the bread is pink with the tomato juice.
4. Sprinkle generously with olive oil and salt and pepper to taste. Serve immediately.

BREAD AND FOCACCIA

Pane e Focaccie

"Per l'affamato, il pane ha sapore di lasagne"—"For the hungry, bread has the flavor of lasagna"—is an old Italian saying. But for me, good bread is even better than lasagna, meat, fish, or any other food.

I love a brown and crusty loaf. I can never understand why some people pull out the center and others cut off the crusts before eating their bread—I enjoy the crunchy crust and soft interior equally. Whole wheat, sourdough, and sesame-seeded Sicilian bread are my special favorites. When the bread is very good, I like it unadorned, although a drizzle of fruity extra-virgin olive oil can't hurt. Nothing satisfies as well and rounds out a meal like bread.

Italians make a wonderful variety of excellent breads. A few of them are made here commercially, but there are some that I prefer to make at home. These are mostly *focaccie*, delicious flatbreads from all over Italy served warm with meals or in-between, plus some unusual loaves like olive bread, unsalted Tuscan bread, and a rich Parmesan bread. Like most breads, these freeze well, so you can make them ahead to have on hand any time.

MAKING BREADS BY MACHINE

Unless noted, the breads in this chapter can be made in a food processor or in a heavy-duty mixer with a dough hook, as well as by hand.

To use the food processor, dissolve the yeast in the warm water in a small bowl. In a food processor fitted with the steel blade, combine the dry ingredients, using the lesser amount of flour given. Process briefly.

Use the amount of liquid ingredients given but at room temperature, not warm, since processors give off heat and you do not want to cook the yeast. Combine the yeast mixture with the liquid ingredients. With the machine running, quickly pour the liquid ingredients through the feed tube. Process for 45

To freeze baked bread or focaccia, cool it completely on a wire rack. Cut the bread into slices or pieces, if desired. Wrap tightly in aluminum foil and place in a plastic bag. Seal and freeze for up to one month. To reheat, remove from the plastic bag and loosen the foil. Bake in a 350°F preheated oven until heated through, about 10 to 30 minutes according to the thickness of the bread. Open the foil completely and bake for 5 minutes longer or until crisp.

TUSCAN BREAD

Pane Toscano

Makes 2 loaves

Tuscan bread has a chewy, crusty exterior and moist interior with large spongelike holes. A combination of bread and whole wheat flours gives a nutty flavor but its most distinctive characteristic is a lack of salt. The bread was traditionally made this way to complement Tuscan foods, which are often quite salty and spicy. If you don't like the unsalted version, you can add up to a tablespoon of salt when adding the flour—it may not be authentically Tuscan but it will still be very good.

Though this bread is very simple to make, the dough is quite sticky and moist. For this reason, it is best to mix the dough in a heavy-duty mixer or a food processor.

Serve Pane Toscano with antipasti or slice it to make crostini (page 145).

1 envelope dry yeast
½ teaspoon sugar
2 cups warm water (105° to 115°F)
4 to 4½ cups unbleached all-purpose flour or bread flour
½ cup whole wheat flour

1. In the large bowl of an electric mixer, sprinkle the yeast and sugar over ½ cup of the water. Let stand for 5 minutes. Stir to dissolve the yeast.

2. Add the remaining water, 4 cups of the all-purpose flour, and the whole wheat flour. Stir to make a soft dough. Knead at low speed for 5 minutes or until the dough is smooth and elastic, adding additional bread flour as needed. The dough should remain somewhat sticky and moist.

3. Oil a large bowl. Add the dough and turn it to oil the top. Cover with a kitchen towel and let stand in a warm draft-free place until doubled in bulk, about 1½ hours.

4. Dust a baking sheet with flour. With floured hands, knead the dough briefly to eliminate air bubbles. Cut the dough into two pieces. Shape each piece into a 14-inch loaf, rolling it between your palms. Place the loaves several inches apart on the baking sheet. Cover loosely with a towel. Let rise for 30 minutes.

5. Preheat the oven to 400°F.

6. Bake the bread until browned and the loaves sound hollow when tapped on the bottom, about 40 minutes. Remove the loaves to a wire rack. Cool completely.

seconds to 1 minute or until the dough forms a ball. The surface will be smooth and the dough will be elastic.

Remove the dough and place it on a lightly floured surface. Knead briefly, adding more flour if too moist. Shape the dough into a ball and let rise as directed.

To use a heavy-duty mixer, dissolve the yeast in the warm water. Add all the ingredients (using the lesser amount of flour) at the temperature given. Mix with the flat paddle until a dough is formed, then switch to the dough hook. Knead for 4 to 5 minutes, adding additional flour as needed, until the dough is smooth and springs back when pinched. Remove the dough from the mixer bowl and knead briefly with your hands on a lightly floured surface. Shape the dough into a ball and let rise as directed.

BREAD-MAKING TIPS

The kind of flour used is very important in bread making. Most of the recipes in this book call for unbleached all-purpose flour or bread flour. These flours are higher in gluten, a protein that makes them stronger and produces firmer, chewier bread. Bleached all-purpose flour is lower in gluten and is usually unsuitable for bread making, unless you want a very tender crumb, as in the Parmesan Bread on page 168.

Since flours vary, it is not possible to give an exact measurement. Sometimes you will need a little more flour, sometimes a little less. Always start with the lesser amount given and add more as needed.

Knowing when to stop

OLIVE BREAD

Pane alle Olive

Makes 2 loaves

Rome's Campo dei Fiore market is one of my all-time favorite places. Every morning except Sunday, makeshift stalls are erected from which an amazing variety of fruits, vegetables, seafood, meats, herbs, housewares, shoes, and flowers are sold. The vendors call out to passing shoppers, offering their wares along with samples, recipes, advice, and loud commentary on whatever subjects happen to come to mind.

I spend hours browsing, chatting with the sellers and shoppers and admiring the fabulous array of foods on display. At one seafood stall five different kinds of squid are sold, another stall features a seasonally changing display of wild mushrooms, while a third sells only olives. By noon, I am more than a little hungry and make my way toward a little bakery tucked behind the flower stall.

The bakery makes a number of excellent breads and simple desserts but one of its biggest attractions for me is a large ring-shaped loaf studded with fat green olives. It has a firm, crunchy outer crust though it is chewy and moist inside and permeated with a rich olive flavor. It is a perfect accompaniment to some good salami, cheese, or just a glass of red wine. Roman housewives stop there too, and buy big chunks of the luscious bread. Needless to say, it disappears rapidly.

If you should visit the Campo dei Fiore, the bakery, simply named "Forno," or "oven," is on the perimeter of the market. Also not to be missed is their outstanding Torta di Ricotta. It consists of a crumbly cookielike crust baked with a thick topping of very fresh, rum-scented ricotta.

The following is my version of Pane alle Olive. Its success depends in large part on the kind of olives that you use. Baking the olives in the bread tends to tame the flavor of even strongly flavored olives. You can use any flavorful, imported olives such as those from Italy or Greece. Use all black or all green or a combination of the two—but don't even think of using tasteless ripe olives from a can.

Make this bread in an electric mixer with a dough hook or by hand. The olives would become too finely chopped in a food processor.

1 package dry yeast
¾ cup warm water (105° to 110°F)
¼ cup extra-virgin olive oil
1¼ cups drained pitted black or green olives, such as Kalamata or Sicilian (about 12 ounces before pitting)
3 to 3¼ cups unbleached all-purpose flour or bread flour

1. In a large bowl, sprinkle the yeast over the warm water. Let stand for 5 minutes.

2. Stir the mixture until the yeast is dissolved. Add the oil, olives, and 3 cups of the flour. Stir until a soft dough forms.

3. On a lightly floured surface, knead the dough until smooth and elastic, about 10 minutes, adding additional flour if the dough feels sticky. Because of the moisture from the olives, the dough will seem soft and moist but don't add more flour than is necessary to make a smooth dough.

4. Place the dough in a large oiled bowl. Turn the dough to oil the top. Cover with a towel and let rise in a warm draft-free place until doubled in bulk, about 1 hour.

5. Oil a large baking sheet. Knead the dough briefly to eliminate air bubbles. Divide the dough into two pieces. Flatten one half to a 1-inch thickness, then roll it up tightly to form a long loaf. Roll the loaf between your palms to even it out. Repeat with the remaining dough. Place the loaves on the prepared baking sheet about 4 inches apart. Cover loosely with a towel and let rise again until doubled in bulk, about 1 hour.

6. Preheat the oven to 400°F.

7. Bake the bread for 35 minutes or until lightly browned and the loaves sound hollow when tapped on the bottom. Remove the loaves from the baking sheet and cool completely on wire racks.

adding flour can be tricky. For most breads, the finished dough should look very smooth and feel moist and only a little sticky. It should also be pliable and elastic—that is, the dough will pull back somewhat when it is pinched. Some breads, such as the Pane Toscano or Focaccia di Patate, are made with a moister dough. Since they are harder to handle, these are best made in an electric mixer or food processor. For most breads, it is better to err on the side of a slightly moister, stickier dough made with less flour than one that is too dry, dense, and heavy from too much flour.

Kneading the dough not only blends the ingredients but helps to develop the gluten that gives the bread its structure. Don't skimp on kneading time. Set a timer to remind you how long you have been at it.

BREADSTICKS

Grissini

Makes about 6 dozen breadsticks

Long skinny breadsticks are great with antipasto. Sometimes I stand them in a decorative crock and set them on the table as an edible centerpiece; other times I just place a small heap of them above each diner's plate, much as they do in Piedmont.

In this recipe, a pasta machine is used to cut the grissini dough into strips. The dough must be quite dry to prevent it from sticking in the machine. As you move the dough from the cutters to the baking sheet, it becomes elongated. The finished breadsticks are very thin and crunchy with a crooked, handmade appearance. They keep well in a sealed container for several weeks.

1 package dry yeast
1 cup warm water (105° to 115°F)
2 tablespoons extra-virgin olive oil
**2½ to 3 cups unbleached all-purpose flour or
  bread flour**
1 teaspoon salt
2 tablespoons yellow cornmeal

1. In a large bowl, sprinkle the yeast over the water. Let stand for 5 minutes.

2. Stir the mixture until the yeast is dissolved. Stir in the olive oil. Add 2 ½ cups of the flour and the salt. Stir until a soft dough forms.

3. On a lightly floured surface, knead the dough until firm and elastic, about 10 minutes, adding additional flour as needed to make a nonsticky dough.

4. Place the dough in a large oiled bowl. Turn the dough to oil the top. Cover with a towel and let rise in a warm draft-free place until doubled in bulk, about 1 hour.

5. Preheat the oven to 350°F. Sprinkle two large baking sheets with cornmeal.

6. Knead the dough briefly to eliminate air bubbles. Divide the dough into six pieces. Flatten one piece of dough into a 5- × 4- × ¼-inch oval. Dust it with additional flour so that it is not sticky. Keep the remaining dough covered.

7. Insert a short end of the dough into the fettucine cutter on a pasta machine and cut the dough into ¼-inch strips. (To cut the dough by hand, flatten it with a rolling pin on a cutting board. Cut into ¼-inch strips with a large heavy knife dipped in flour.) Arrange the strips ½ inch apart on one of the prepared baking sheets. Repeat with the remaining dough.

8. Bake for 20 to 25 minutes or until lightly browned. Cool on wire racks.

Grissini all'Erbe　Add 2 teaspoons dried oregano along with the flour.

SARDINIAN FLAT BREAD

Carta da Musica

Makes 6 large breads

Making this irresistibly crunchy bread from Sardinia requires some patience since the dough must be rolled as thin as possible, as thin as a sheet of music paper.

The bread keeps well for several weeks. Break the sheets into smaller pieces for storage.

**1¼ to 1½ cups unbleached all-purpose flour or
bread flour
1¼ cups fine semolina flour
1 teaspoon salt
1 cup water**

1. In a large bowl, combine 1 ¼ cups of the all-purpose flour, the semolina flour, and salt. Stir in the water until the mixture forms a soft dough.

2. On a lightly floured surface, knead the dough, adding additional flour as necessary to form a stiff dough. Knead until smooth and elastic, about 5 minutes. Wrap the dough in plastic wrap and let rest at room temperature for 1 hour.

3. Preheat the oven to 450°F. Divide the dough into six pieces. Roll out one piece of dough to a 12- × 9-inch rectangle. It should be thin enough so that you can see your hand through it. Lay the dough on an ungreased baking sheet. It does not matter if the dough is not perfectly shaped. Just be sure that it lies flat with no wrinkles.

4. Bake until the top of the bread is just firm, about 2 minutes. Turn and bake the other side until lightly browned, about 2 minutes more.

5. Transfer the bread to a wire rack to cool. Repeat with the remaining dough. To serve, break each sheet into 4 or more pieces.

SEASONED CARTA DA MUSICA

Carta da Musica all'Olio

At a Sardinian dinner at the Union Square Cafe in New York to benefit the American Institute of Wine and Food, *Carta da Musica* was served warm, drizzled with extra-virgin olive oil and sprinkled with coarse salt. It is delicious with salads or cheese.

1 sheet Carta da Musica (see page 164)
2 tablespoons extra-virgin olive oil
Coarse salt

1. Preheat the oven to 350°F.
2. Place the bread on an ungreased baking sheet and heat for 5 minutes or just until warm. Break the bread into 6 or more pieces. Stack the pieces on a plate, drizzling each layer with oil and sprinkling with salt. Serve warm.

PROSCIUTTO BREAD

Pane al Prosciutto

Makes 2 loaves

2 packages dry yeast
1½ cups warm water (105° to 115°F)
⅓ cup extra-virgin olive oil
3½ to 4 cups unbleached all-purpose flour or bread flour
1 teaspoon salt
1 teaspoon minced fresh garlic
1 teaspoon coarsely ground black pepper
8 ounces prosciutto, sliced ¼ inch thick, diced (or use a combination of prosciutto and salami)
1 cup coarsely chopped provolone (about 4 ounces)
1 egg yolk beaten with 1 tablespoon water

1. In a large bowl, sprinkle the yeast over ½ cup of the warm water. Let stand for 5 minutes.

2. Stir the mixture until the yeast is dissolved. Stir in the remaining 1 cup water, the oil, 2 cups of the flour, the salt, garlic, and pepper until well blended.

3. Stir in the prosciutto, cheese, and enough additional flour to make a soft dough. Transfer the dough to a lightly floured surface and knead until smooth and elastic, about 12 minutes. Add additional flour as necessary to make a stiff dough.

4. Oil a large bowl and place the dough in it, turning it to oil the top. Cover with a towel and let rise in a warm draft-free place until doubled in bulk, about 2 hours.

5. Oil a large baking sheet. Punch the dough down and divide it into four pieces. Roll each piece into a 24-inch rope. Twist two of the ropes together, then form them into a circle. Pinch the ends together to seal. Repeat with the remaining dough. Place the circles on the baking sheet 2 inches apart. Cover with a towel and let rise in a warm draft-free place until doubled in bulk, about 1 hour.

6. Preheat the oven to 400°F.

7. Brush the beaten egg yolk over the risen loaves. Bake for 30 minutes or until golden brown. Cool on wire racks.

CRISP FENNEL RINGS

Taralli

Makes 4 dozen rings

In Apulia, these crunchy rings are ubiquitous at meals, with wine or cheese before or after a meal, or as a snack. They keep well in a tightly closed tin for several weeks.

1 package dry yeast

1 cup warm water (105° to 110°F)

3 cups unbleached all-purpose flour or bread flour

2 tablespoons fennel seeds

1½ teaspoons salt

⅓ cup extra-virgin olive oil

1. In a large bowl, sprinkle the yeast over the water. Let stand for 5 minutes.

2. Stir the mixture until the yeast is dissolved. Stir in the flour, fennel seeds, salt, and olive oil. Turn the dough out onto a lightly floured surface and knead until smooth and elastic, about 10 minutes.

3. Place the dough in an oiled bowl. Turn to oil the top. Cover with a towel and let rise in a warm draft-free place until doubled in bulk, about 2 hours.

4. Preheat the oven to 375°F. Knead the dough briefly to eliminate air bubbles. Divide it into four parts, then cut each part into twelve pieces. Roll one piece between your palms into a 6-inch rope. Pinch the ends together to form a ring. Repeat with the remaining dough. Place the rings on large ungreased baking sheets 1 inch apart.

5. Bake for 45 minutes or until browned and crisp. Cool on wire racks.

Taralli al Pepe Substitute 1 teaspoon coarsely ground black pepper for the fennel seeds.

PARMESAN BREAD

Pane al Parmigiano

Makes 2 loaves

A tender golden-colored bread to serve with antipasto, soup, or salad. It is also good toasted and spread with sweet butter or olive oil. All-purpose flour gives it a tender, cakelike interior.

1 package dry yeast
1 cup warm water (105° to 115°F)
1 large egg, lightly beaten
2 tablespoons unsalted butter, melted
3 cups unbleached all-purpose flour
1 cup freshly grated Parmigiano-Reggiano
½ teaspoon salt
1 egg white, lightly beaten

1. In a large bowl, sprinkle the yeast over the water. Let stand for 5 minutes.

2. Stir the mixture until the yeast is dissolved. Stir in the egg and butter. Add the flour, cheese, and salt. Stir until a stiff dough forms. Transfer the dough to a lightly floured surface and knead until smooth and elastic, about 10 minutes.

3. Place the dough in a large buttered bowl. Turn to butter the top. Cover with a towel. Let rise in a warm draft-free place until the dough has doubled in bulk, about 2 hours.

4. Butter a large baking sheet. Knead the dough lightly to eliminate air bubbles. Divide the dough in half and shape it into two round loaves. Place the loaves on the prepared baking sheet. Cover loosely with a towel and let rise until doubled in bulk, about 1 hour.

5. Preheat the oven to 425°F.

6. Brush the loaves with the egg white and slash the tops with a razor or sharp knife. Bake the loaves until browned, 25 to 30 minutes. Cool completely on wire racks.

PARMESAN WALNUT WAFERS

Biscotti al Parmigiano e alle Noci

Makes 48 biscuits

We were served biscuits like these as we pondered the menu choices at Le Tre Vaselle, an inn and restaurant in Torgiano near Perugia. They are just the thing to nibble with a glass of spumante or red wine.

1¼ cups unbleached all-purpose flour
4 ounces freshly grated Parmigiano-Reggiano
¼ teaspoon salt
8 tablespoons (1 stick) chilled unsalted butter, cut into ½-inch pieces
½ cup walnuts, toasted and finely chopped
2 tablespoons milk
1 large egg

1. In a bowl, combine the flour, cheese, and salt. With a pastry blender or a fork, blend in the butter until the mixture resembles coarse crumbs. Stir in the nuts.

2. In a small bowl, beat together the milk and the egg. Pour the egg mixture over the dry ingredients and stir just until blended. Shape the dough into a ball.

3. Cut the dough into two equal pieces. Shape each piece into a 7-inch log and place each on a piece of plastic wrap. Wrap tightly and refrigerate until firm, at least 4 hours or overnight.

4. Preheat the oven to 400°F. Butter two large baking sheets.

5. Cut the logs into ¼-inch slices and arrange the slices 1 inch apart on the prepared baking sheets. Bake until the biscuits are lightly browned around the edges, 10 to 12 minutes. Transfer to wire racks to cool.

WHOLE WHEAT SCHIACCIATA

Schiacciata Nera

Serves 8

We once rented a little house on the outskirts of Florence, and the owner, a very charming lady who lived next door, would stop in occasionally with advice, questions, and, once in a while, something to eat. One day she brought an unusual flat bread with a shiny crust studded with coarse salt and a soft chewy center. It was laced with nuggets of whole wheat and had a satisfying nutty flavor. The bread was baked only on Mondays and Wednesdays, she explained, and every Monday and Wednesday thereafter we went to the bakery to buy some ourselves. Schiacciata, meaning "squashed" is the Tuscan name for focaccia.

The dough for this schiacciata is a bit complicated. It is made with a starter, a soft mixture of yeast and flour that gives the bread a greater depth of flavor and makes it possible to use less yeast.

The nutty wheat flavor and texture come from whole wheat flour and bulgur, coarsely ground wheat berries that must be soaked to soften them.

1 teaspoon (about ½ package) dry yeast
1½ cups plus ⅓ cup warm water (105° to 115°F)
2½ to 3 cups bread flour or unbleached all-
**   purpose flour**
½ cup (about 3 ounces) medium bulgur wheat
½ cup whole wheat flour
1 teaspoon fine salt
¼ cup olive oil
1 egg white, beaten
Coarse salt

1. In a medium bowl, sprinkle the yeast over the 1½ cups warm water. Let stand for 5 minutes. Stir the mixture to dissolve the yeast thoroughly. Stir in 1 cup of the bread flour until well blended and a very soft dough is formed. Transfer this starter to an oiled bowl. Cover with a towel and let rise in a warm draft-free place until doubled in bulk, about 2 hours.

2. Meanwhile, in a small bowl, soak the bulgur in 1 cup warm water for 1 hour. Drain. (This can be soaked overnight in the refrigerator.)

3. In a large bowl, combine the whole wheat flour, 1½ cups of the remaining bread flour, and the 1 teaspoon fine salt. Add the starter, drained bulgur, olive oil, and the ⅓ cup warm water. Knead the mixture until it is smooth and elastic, about 10 minutes, adding more flour as necessary. The dough should be slightly sticky.

4. Oil a large bowl and add the dough, turning to oil the top. Cover with a towel and let rise in a warm draft-free place until doubled in bulk, about 2 hours.

5. Oil a 15- × 10- × 1-inch jelly-roll pan. On a lightly floured surface, knead the dough briefly to eliminate air bubbles. Flatten the dough and place it in the prepared pan. Stretch and pat the dough to fit the pan comfortably, building it up slightly along the sides. Cover with a towel and let rise until doubled in bulk, about 1 hour.

6. Preheat the oven to 400°F.

7. With your fingertips, press the dough at 1-inch intervals to make dimples. Brush the surface lightly with the beaten egg white and sprinkle lightly with coarse salt. Bake for 25 to 30 minutes or until browned and crisp. Slide onto a rack to cool. Serve warm or cooled, cut into squares.

BASIC FOCACCIA DOUGH

Pasta per Focaccia

Makes 25 slices

1 package dry yeast
1 cup warm water (105° to 115°F)
¼ cup extra-virgin olive oil
3 to 3½ cups unbleached all-purpose flour or bread flour
½ teaspoon salt

1. In a large bowl, sprinkle the yeast over the water. Let stand for 5 minutes.

2. Stir the mixture until the yeast is dissolved. Add the olive oil. Add 3 cups of the flour and the salt. Stir the mixture until a soft dough forms. Turn the dough out onto a lightly floured surface. Knead until smooth and elastic, about 10 minutes, adding more flour if the dough feels sticky.

3. Oil a large bowl and place the dough in it, turning it once to oil the top. Cover with a towel and let rise in a warm draft-free place until doubled in bulk, about 2 hours.

4. Proceed with any of the focaccia recipes.

CHEESE AND TOMATO DUMPLINGS

Panzerotti Pugliesi

Makes about 2 dozen dumplings

In Apulia, these little turnovers are often deep fried, but I prefer them baked. They have a tendency to pop open while baking, so be sure to seal them tightly. Even if they do open, they will still look quite pretty and taste delicious.

**3 plum tomatoes (about 8 ounces) or 1 large
 tomato**
Salt
4 ounces fresh mozzarella, finely chopped
½ cup freshly grated Pecorino Romano
Freshly ground black pepper
1 recipe Basic Focaccia Dough (see page 172)

1. Bring a medium saucepan of water to a boil. Drop in the tomatoes and simmer for 30 seconds. Immediately drain the tomatoes and let cool. Cut them in half and slip off the skins. Scoop out the seeds. Finely chop the tomatoes. Place them in a colander set over a plate and sprinkle with salt. Let drain for 30 minutes.

2. In a bowl, combine the tomatoes, cheeses, and pepper to taste.

3. Preheat the oven to 450°F.

4. Cut the dough in half and roll out one piece to a ¼-inch thickness. With a 3-inch round biscuit or cookie cutter, cut the dough into circles. Place a tablespoonful of the tomato mixture in the center of each circle. Moisten the edge of the dough and fold it over to enclose the filling and form a semicircle. With a fork, press the edges firmly together to seal.

5. Arrange the panzerotti on a large ungreased baking sheet about 1 inch apart. Pierce them with a fork once or twice to allow steam to escape. Bake the panzerotti until golden brown and puffed, about 20 minutes. Let cool slightly.

PROSCIUTTO-STUFFED FOCACCIA

Focaccia Ripiena di Prosciutto

Serves 6

The possibilities for fillings for this focaccia are endless. Think of it as a giant hero sandwich and try stuffing it with mortadella or salami, mozzarella with tomatoes and basil, anchovies with roasted peppers, sautéed greens with garlic and olive oil, grilled or fried eggplant slices, etc.

This focaccia makes great picnic food.

1 recipe Basic Focaccia Dough (see page 172)
¼ cup extra-virgin olive oil
Coarse salt
8 ounces thinly sliced prosciutto
Freshly ground black pepper

1. Preheat the oven to 450°F. Oil a 12-inch round pizza pan.
2. Roll or pat the dough out to fit the prepared pan. With your fingertips, dimple the surface. Drizzle with 2 tablespoons of the olive oil. Sprinkle lightly with salt.
3. Bake the focaccia until puffed and golden, about 35 minutes. Transfer the focaccia to a cutting board. With a large serrated knife, carefully split the focaccia crosswise into two layers. Remove the top layer and arrange the prosciutto slices on the bottom layer. Sprinkle with pepper to taste. Drizzle with the remaining 2 tablespoons olive oil. Replace the top and cut into wedges to serve. Serve warm or at room temperature.

FOCACCIA STUFFED WITH TOMATOES AND ANCHOVIES

Focaccia Ripiena di Pomodori

Serves 6 to 8

My Uncle Carl lived in a Brooklyn cold-water flat with an enormous cast-iron coal stove. He loved to cook and one of his specialties was a pizza similar to this. I can still recall the sight and smell of the enormous pans of dough rising near the warmth of the stove.

¼ cup extra-virgin olive oil

2 medium onions peeled and thinly sliced

1 28-ounce can peeled Italian tomatoes, drained and chopped

2 tablespoons capers, drained

1 teaspoon dried oregano

Salt and freshly ground black pepper

1 recipe Basic Focaccia Dough (see page 172)

1 2-ounce can anchovy fillets, drained

½ cup imported black olives, preferably Kalamata, pitted and chopped

¼ cup freshly grated imported Pecorino Romano

1. In a large skillet, heat the oil. Add the onions and cook over medium heat until tender and golden, 10 to 15 minutes.

2. Add the tomatoes, capers, oregano, and salt and pepper to taste. Simmer, stirring occasionally, until the tomato juices have evaporated and the sauce is very thick, about 10 minutes. Let cool.

3. Preheat the oven to 450°F. Oil a 12-inch pizza pan.

4. Divide the dough into two pieces. Roll out one piece of dough to a 12-inch circle and place it in the prepared pan. Spread the dough with the sauce, leaving a 1-inch border all around. Arrange the anchovies over the sauce. Sprinkle with the olives and cheese.

5. Roll out the remaining dough to a 12-inch circle and place it over the filling. Press the edges of the dough together to seal well.

6. Bake until golden brown, about 30 minutes. Serve warm or at room temperature.

CHEESE-STUFFED FOCACCIA

Focaccia al Formaggio

Serves 8

This very old recipe comes from Restaurant "La Manuelina" in Recco on the Ligurian coast. The original version supposedly was developed centuries ago when pirates frequently raided the coastal towns. The inhabitants were forced to flee inland, where grain was milled into flour and flocks of sheep grazed. Hungry, they used the flour and locally made sheep's milk cheese to make a quick but nourishing food. Manuelina, the original proprietor of the restaurant that still bears her name, adapted the idea to modern times and it became a much-duplicated local specialty.

The unusual dough, which uses no leavening, is delightfully crisp and crackling when baked. Extra patience is required to roll it as thin as required, so allow enough time.

The cheese used in Liguria, called *formagetta del tipo classico ligure*, is not available here. Stracchino cheese is a good alternative, but this, too, may be hard to locate. Otherwise, a combination of fresh goat cheese and ricotta is a credible substitute.

3 cups unbleached all-purpose flour or bread flour
1 teaspoon salt
¾ cup water
5 tablespoons extra-virgin olive oil
1 pound stracchino cheese, rind removed, or 8 ounces (1 cup) ricotta cheese and 8 ounces fresh goat cheese
Coarse salt

1. In a large bowl, combine the flour and salt. Add the water and 4 tablespoons of the oil. Stir until the mixture forms a soft dough.

2. Turn the dough out onto a lightly floured surface and knead until smooth and elastic, about 10 minutes. Cut the dough in half. Cover each piece with plastic wrap and set aside to rest for at least 30 minutes.

3. Preheat the oven to 400°F. Lightly brush a 15- × 10- × 1-inch jelly-roll pan with olive oil. Slice the stracchino thinly, or, if using the ricotta and goat cheese, whisk the two together until blended.

4. On a lightly floured surface, roll out one piece of the dough to a 17- × 12-inch rectangle. Drape the dough over the rolling pin and lay it in the prepared pan. Dot small spoonfuls of the cheese over the surface of the dough, leaving a 1-inch border all around.

5. Roll out the remaining dough to a 17- × 12-inch rectangle and place it over the cheese. Pat the dough with your fingertips to eliminate air bubbles and form dimples on the surface. Fold the border of the bottom dough over the top. Press firmly to seal.

6. Brush the surface with the remaining 1 tablespoon olive oil. With a fork, pierce the dough at 1-inch intervals. Sprinkle lightly with coarse salt. Bake on the lowest oven rack for 30 minutes or until the top is golden brown with darker bubbles of dough. Let cool for 5 minutes. Cut into squares.

POTATO FOCACCIA

Focaccia di Patate

Makes 25 slices

This bread is from Apulia, where potatoes are used more frequently than in most other region of Italy.

1¼ pounds baking potatoes, peeled and cut into 1-inch chunks
1 package dry yeast
3 tablespoons warm water (105° to 115°F)
¼ cup extra-virgin olive oil
4½ cups unbleached all-purpose flour or bread flour
2 teaspoons salt
1 tablespoon chopped fresh rosemary or 1 teaspoon crumbled dried

1. Place the potatoes in a medium saucepan and add water to cover. Bring to a simmer over medium heat and cook until tender when pierced with a fork, about 20 minutes. Drain the potatoes, reserving ½ cup of the cooking liquid. Mash the potatoes with a masher or by passing them through a food mill or ricer.

2. In the large bowl of a heavy-duty electric mixer, sprinkle the yeast over the 3 tablespoons water. Let stand for 5 minutes. Stir the mixture until the yeast is dissolved. Stir in the potatoes, the reserved cooking liquid, and 2 tablespoons of the olive oil.

3. Blend in the flour and salt. Knead at low speed for 5 minutes or until the dough is smooth and elastic.

4. Oil a large bowl and scrape the dough into it. Cover with a towel and let rise in a warm draft-free place until doubled in bulk, about 2 hours.

5. Oil a 15- × 10- × 1-inch jelly-roll pan. Stir the dough down and scrape it into the pan. With floured hands, pat the dough out to fit the pan evenly. Cover loosely and let rise for 1 hour.

6. Preheat the oven to 450°F.

7. Make dimples in the dough at 1-inch intervals with your fingertips. Sprinkle the dough with the remaining 2 tablespoons oil and the rosemary. Bake for 20 to 25 minutes or until puffed and golden brown. Slide the bread onto a rack to cool slightly. Cut into 3- × 2-inch rectangles. Serve warm.

ONION FOCACCIA

Fitascetta

Makes 25 slices

Sometimes spelled *filascetta*, this rustic bread is Lombardy's version of focaccia.

4 tablespoons unsalted butter
1½ pounds red onions (about 4 medium), peeled and thinly sliced
1 teaspoon sugar
½ teaspoon salt
Freshly ground black pepper
1 recipe Basic Focaccia Dough (see page 172)

1. In a large skillet, melt the butter over medium-low heat. Add the onions and cook, stirring occasionally, until very tender but not browned, about 30 minutes. Stir in the sugar, salt, and pepper to taste. Let cool.

2. Oil a 15- × 10- × 1-inch jelly-roll pan. Turn the dough out onto a lightly floured surface and knead briefly to eliminate air bubbles. Stretch and pat the dough out to fit the prepared pan. Cover loosely with a towel and let rise in a warm draft-free place for 30 minutes.

3. Preheat the oven to 450°F.

4. Spread the onions over the dough. Bake for 15 minutes. Lower the heat to 375°F and bake for 15 to 20 minutes until the bread is golden brown. Cut into 3- × 2-inch rectangles. Serve warm.

SEMOLINA FOCACCIA

Focaccia di Semolina

Serves 8

Off-season in Rapallo on the Italian Riviera is a lovely, quiet time. There are few tourists, and many businesses are open only during the booming summer season. Naturally, I was surprised to see a crowd waiting impatiently outside a tiny bakery. A delicious aroma of fresh bread beckoned from within. Curious, I waited too and was rewarded with a large square of warm focaccia. It was golden colored and denser than the usual focaccia and left big oily stains on the coarse paper in which it was wrapped. It was so good that the next day I went back for more. I learned that the wonderfully crunchy texture came from semolina flour, the kind used for making pasta.

As a variation, try sprinkling this focaccia with chopped fresh sage or rosemary instead of salt.

1 package dry yeast
¼ cup warm water (105° to 115°F)
1¼ cups warm milk (105° to 115°F)
6 tablespoons olive oil
3 to 3½ cups unbleached all-purpose flour or
  bread flour
1 cup fine semolina flour
1 teaspoon fine salt
Coarse salt

1. In a large bowl, sprinkle the yeast over the water. Let stand for 5 minutes.

2. Stir to dissolve the yeast. Stir in the milk and 3 tablespoons of the olive oil. Add 3 cups of the all-purpose flour, the semolina, and fine salt. Stir until a soft dough forms.

3. Turn the dough out onto a lightly floured surface and knead until smooth and elastic, about 10 minutes, adding additional flour as needed.

4. Place the dough in a large oiled bowl. Turn the dough to grease the top. Cover loosely with a towel and let rise in a warm draft-free place until doubled in bulk, about 1½ hours.

5. Oil a 15- × 10- × 1-inch jelly-roll pan. Knead the dough briefly to eliminate air bubbles. Stretch and pat the dough out to fit the pan. Cover with a towel and let rise for 1 hour.

6. Dimple the dough with your fingertips. Brush the surface with the remaining 3 tablespoons olive oil. Sprinkle lightly with coarse salt. Bake for 25 to 30 minutes or until golden. Cut into squares and serve warm.

GORGONZOLA FOCACCIA

Focaccia al Gorgonzola

Makes 25 slices

Tangy rivers of Gorgonzola are streaked throughout this focaccia.

6 ounces imported Italian Gorgonzola
1 recipe Basic Focaccia Dough (see page 172)

1. Cut off the rind of the Gorgonzola and mash the cheese coarsely with a fork.

2. Oil a 15- × 10- × 1-inch jelly-roll pan. On a lightly floured surface, knead the dough a few times to eliminate air bubbles. Knead in the Gorgonzola just until lightly distributed throughout the dough. The cheese should remain chunky.

3. Stretch and pat the dough out to fit the prepared pan. Cover with a towel and let rise in a warm draft-free place for 30 minutes.

4. Preheat the oven to 400°F.

5. Bake the focaccia for 25 minutes or until golden. Slide a metal spatula under the focaccia to loosen it from the pan and transfer it to a cutting board. Cut into 3- × 2-inch rectangles. Serve warm.

OLIVE AND ROSEMARY FOCACCIA

Focaccia alle Olive e al Rosmarino

Makes 25 slices

Rosemary and olives have a natural affinity for one another.

1 recipe Basic Focaccia Dough (see page 172)
½ cup sliced pitted imported black olives, such as Kalamata
1 tablespoon fresh rosemary, chopped, or 1 teaspoon dried rosemary, crushed

1. Oil a 15- × 10- × 1-inch jelly-roll pan. On a lightly floured surface, knead the dough a few times to eliminate air bubbles. Knead in the olives and rosemary.

2. Stretch and pat the dough out to fit into the prepared pan. Cover with a towel and let rise in a warm draft-free place for 30 minutes.

3. Preheat the oven to 400°F.

4. Bake the focaccia for 25 minutes or until golden. Cut into 3- × 2-inch rectangles. Serve warm.

RICE, PASTA, AND POLENTA

Riso, Pasta, e Polenta

Of all the times I have eaten antipasti in Italy, I can recall only two occasions when pasta was among them, once as a stuffing for peppers (page 62) and another served at room temperature as a salad (page 194). Though Italians love their pasta, it is reserved for a first course or sometimes a main course, rarely as antipasto.

Rice, on the other hand, is frequently served as an antipasto, either as a stuffing for seafood or vegetables or as a salad, fried in little balls or pancakes, or baked into tortes and crostatas.

I use two kinds of rice for antipasti. For salads, I prefer long-grain rice, since the grains remain separate and not sticky. For stuffings, I prefer Italian short-grain rice such as Arborio or Vialone Nano. Short-grain rice is stickier and creamier so it stays together better in a filling.

Though crostini are usually made with toasted bread, they can also be made with slices of crisped polenta.

Meglio pasta e

fagioli a casa

propria che pizza

dolce a casa

degli altri.

Better pasta and

beans in your own

home than cake at

the home of others.

SUMMER RICE SALAD

Insalata di Riso Estiva

Serves 8

Rice salads are very popular in Italy in the summer. Some are carefully constructed of fresh ingredients while others are a catchall for leftovers or store-bought ingredients. Either way, I have never met one that I did not like.

Use this recipe as a guide, varying it by substituting chicken, tuna, eggs, or ham for the prosciutto, and radishes, cucumbers, green beans, and tomatoes for the vegetables.

The salad is best when made the same day it is to be served. Long chilling may cause the rice grains to harden.

1½ cups long-grain rice
Salt
2 medium carrots, shredded
1 small zucchini, diced
1 small red bell pepper, cored, seeded, and diced
½ cup finely chopped red onion
4 ounces sliced prosciutto, cut into thin strips
1 cup chopped fresh basil or flat-leaf parsley
½ cup sliced pitted green olives
½ cup extra-virgin olive oil
¼ cup white wine vinegar
Freshly ground black pepper
¼ cup toasted pine nuts

1. In a large saucepan bring 3¼ cups water to a boil. Stir in the rice and 1 teaspoon salt. When the water returns to the boil, stir again. Reduce the heat to low. Cover and cook for 18 to 20 minutes or until the rice is tender. Transfer the rice to a large bowl and let cool slightly.

2. Stir in the vegetables, prosciutto, basil, and olives. Cover and chill for 2 hours.

3. Just before serving, whisk together the oil, vinegar, and salt and pepper to taste. Pour over the salad. Add the pine nuts and toss.

RICE AND ROASTED PEPPER SALAD

Insalata di Riso e Peperoni

Serves 4 to 6

An easy, colorful salad that goes well with many seafood and egg antipasti.

1 cup long-grain rice
Salt
10 fresh basil leaves
2 red bell peppers, roasted, peeled, and seeded
  (see pages 30–33), cut into thin strips
¼ cup extra-virgin olive oil
Freshly ground black pepper

1. In a medium saucepan, bring 2½ cups water to a simmer. Add the rice and salt to taste. Cover and cook until tender, about 18 to 20 minutes.

2. Stack the basil leaves and cut them into thin strips. Drain the peppers and cut them into small squares.

3. In a bowl, combine the rice, basil, peppers, olive oil, and salt and pepper to taste. Toss well. Chill for 1 to 2 hours. Taste for seasoning and serve.

SEAFOOD RICE SALAD

Insalata di Riso Marinara

Serves 8

Swordfish grow to be enormous and markets in Italy always display them with the head and sword attached for easy identification. It can be quite an awesome sight.

Some of the best swordfish in the world comes from Sicily and the Sicilians know dozens of ways to prepare it. In this salad, the rice is cooked in the fish juices to absorb all the flavors.

1 pound squid, cleaned (see page 218)
2 pounds mussels, cleaned and debearded (see page 200)
Salt
1 8-ounce swordfish steak
8 ounces medium shrimp, peeled and deveined
2 cups long-grain rice
½ cup extra-virgin olive oil
4 to 6 tablespoons fresh lemon juice
Freshly ground black pepper
1 large red bell pepper, diced
2 tender celery ribs, chopped
1 large tomato, seeded and diced
1 cup diced peeled cucumber
¼ cup chopped flat-leaf parsley
¼ cup chopped fresh basil

1. Cut the body of the squid into ½-inch rings. Leave the tentacles whole. Drain well and pat dry.

2. Place the mussels in a large pot. Cover and cook over medium heat until the shells open, about 4 minutes, shaking the pan once or twice; remove the mussels from the pot as they open. Cook any unopened mussels a few minutes longer, then discard any that refuse to open.

3. Add 4 cups of water to the mussel juices left in the pot. Bring the water to a simmer and add 1 teaspoon salt. Add the swordfish and cook for 2 minutes. Add the shrimp and cook for 1 minute after the water returns to the simmer. Add the squid and cook just until opaque, about 30 seconds. Drain the fish in a large colander set over a bowl. Strain the cooking liquid through a fine strainer lined with cheesecloth.

4. In a medium saucepan, bring 5 cups of the cooking liquid to a boil over medium heat. Add the rice and return to the boil. Stir the rice, reduce the heat to low, cover, and cook until tender and all the liquid has been absorbed, about 20 minutes. Transfer the rice to a large bowl.

5. In a small bowl, combine the olive oil, 4 tablespoons lemon juice, and salt and pepper to taste. Drizzle half the dressing over the rice. Let cool, stirring occasionally.

6. Cut the swordfish into ½-inch cubes. Shell the shrimp and mussels. Toss the squid, swordfish, shrimp, and mussels with the remaining dressing.

7. When the rice is cool, stir in the seafood and all the remaining ingredients. Chill for 1 to 2 hours. Taste for seasoning just before serving and add additional lemon juice if desired.

RICE AND CRANBERRY BEAN SALAD

Insalata di Riso con i Borlotti

Serves 6

Use pink beans or red kidney beans if cranberry beans are not available.

1 cup long-grain rice
Salt
2 cups drained cooked cranberry beans (see page 74) or 1 19-ounce can cranberry beans, rinsed and drained
⅓ cup finely chopped scallions
2 tablespoons chopped flat-leaf parsley
⅓ cup extra-virgin olive oil
2 tablespoons fresh lemon juice
Freshly ground black pepper
2-ounce piece of Parmigiano-Reggiano

1. In a medium saucepan, bring 2½ cups of water to a boil. Stir in the rice and 1 teaspoon salt. When the water returns to the boil, stir again. Reduce the heat to low. Cover and cook for 18 to 20 minutes or until the rice is tender. Transfer the rice to a serving bowl. Stir in the beans, scallions, and parsley. Let cool.
2. Just before serving, whisk together the oil, lemon juice, and salt and pepper to taste. Pour over the salad and toss well. With a vegetable peeler, shave the Parmigiano into very thin "scales." Scatter the cheese over the salad.

SEMOLINA SALAD

Insalata di Semolina

Serves 4 to 6

Semolina is used mainly for making certain types of Italian pasta and bread, so I was surprised to come across this salad among the antipasto choices at the Trattoria Il Pennello in Florence. Once I tasted it, I realized that it was a takeoff on a classic Tuscan antipasto, *panzanella*. Panzanella is a salad made with day-old Tuscan bread moistened with water, then combined with vegetables and a dressing. The semolina works beautifully, especially since I rarely have day-old Tuscan bread to spare.

1 cup coarse semolina (couscous)
Salt
¼ cup extra-virgin olive oil
2 tablespoons red wine vinegar
Freshly ground black pepper
1 large ripe tomato, cored, seeded, and diced
½ cup chopped peeled cucumber
¼ cup chopped red onion
2 tablespoons chopped fresh basil or flat-leaf parsley

1. In a medium saucepan, bring 1½ cups of water to a boil. Add the semolina and 1 teaspoon salt. Cover and cook for 5 minutes or until the water is evaporated. Transfer the semolina to a large bowl.
2. In a small bowl, whisk together the oil, vinegar, and salt and pepper to taste. Pour over the semolina and stir well. Let cool to room temperature.
3. Stir in the vegetables and basil. Serve immediately.

SAVORY RICE TART

Crostata di Riso

Serves 8

One of my favorite Italian desserts is a sort of custardy rice pudding baked in tender pie crust. In Venice, one pastry shop makes it in a large sheet pan. The portions are cut into big squares and served warm with steaming espresso. In Parma, the same dessert is made in deep individual oval timbale molds.

But the Parmigiani also make a savory version, perfect with a glass of dry spumante. Naturally, it features Parmigiano-Reggiano, the locally made and aptly named "king of cheeses."

Dough

1¼ cups all-purpose flour
¼ cup freshly grated Parmigiano-Reggiano
8 tablespoons (1 stick) unsalted butter, chilled and cut into bits
3½ to 4 tablespoons ice water

Filling

½ cup Arborio or other short-grain rice
1 teaspoon salt
1 cup ricotta
¾ cup freshly grated Parmigiano-Reggiano
2 large eggs
½ cup milk
2 tablespoons unsalted butter, at room temperature
Pinch of freshly grated nutmeg
Pinch of freshly ground black pepper

1. To make the dough, in a large bowl, combine the flour and Parmigiano. Cut in the butter with a pastry blender or two knives

held scissor fashion until the mixture resembles coarse crumbs. Add the ice water a tablespoon at a time and toss with a fork until the flour is evenly moistened and can be pressed together gently to form a dough. Wrap the dough in plastic wrap and refrigerate for at least 1 hour or overnight.

2. On a lightly floured surface, roll out the dough to a 13-inch circle. Drape the dough over the rolling pin and transfer it to an 11-inch tart pan with a removable bottom. Press the dough into the pan and up the sides without stretching it. Trim off all but a ½-inch overhang. Fold in the overhang and press it against the side of the pan. Chill for 30 minutes.

3. Preheat the oven to 400°F.

4. Butter a 14-inch piece of aluminum foil. Line the pastry shell with the foil, buttered side down. Fill the shell with pie weights or dried beans. Bake the shell on the lowest rack of the preheated oven for 10 minutes. Remove the foil and weights and prick the bottom of the shell all over with a fork. Bake for 5 to 8 minutes more or until the pastry is just set and the edges are lightly golden. Cool on a wire rack.

5. Reduce the oven temperature to 375°F.

6. To make the filling, in a medium saucepan, bring 4 cups of water to a boil and add the rice and salt. Return to the boil and cook for 8 minutes. Drain well.

7. In a large bowl, whisk together the ricotta, Parmigiano, eggs, milk, butter, nutmeg, and pepper. Stir in the rice. Pour the mixture into the prepared shell. Bake until golden and slightly puffed, about 30 minutes. Serve warm.

SPINACH AND RICE TORTE

Torta di Spinaci e Riso

Serves 6 to 8

Rice has been cultivated in Piedmont in Northern Italy since the tenth century. In fact, Thomas Jefferson was so impressed by the quality of Italian rice that he wanted to bring some samples home to America with him. Exportation of seeds from Italy was against the law, but Jefferson managed to smuggle out a few sacks with him.

This torte can be cut into wedges to be eaten with a fork or into bite-size squares.

1 pound spinach, washed and stemmed
⅔ cup rice, preferably Arborio or other short-grained Italian rice
1 teaspoon salt
4 tablespoons unsalted butter
1 medium onion, peeled and finely chopped
3 large eggs
½ cup heavy cream
¾ cup freshly grated Parmigiano-Reggiano
¼ teaspoon freshly grated nutmeg
¼ teaspoon freshly ground black pepper

1. Preheat the oven to 350°F. Butter a 9-inch pie pan.
2. Place the spinach in a large pot with just the water that clings to the leaves after washing. Cover and cook over medium-low heat just until wilted, 2 to 3 minutes. Drain and cool. Squeeze out as much water as possible. Finely chop the spinach. Place it in a large bowl.
3. In a medium saucepan, bring 4 cups of water to a boil. Stir in the rice and salt. Return to the boil and cook for 8 minutes. Drain well and transfer to the bowl with the spinach. Stir in 2 tablespoons of the butter.

4. In a small skillet, melt the remaining 2 tablespoons butter over medium heat. Add the onion and cook until tender and golden, about 10 minutes. Scrape the onion into the bowl with the spinach mixture and stir well.

5. In a bowl, beat together the eggs, cream, cheese, nutmeg, and pepper. Stir into the spinach mixture, then spoon into the prepared pan, levelling the top.

6. Bake for 30 minutes or until the edges are lightly browned and a knife inserted into the center comes out clean. Serve hot or at room temperature.

SPAGHETTINI AND MELON SALAD

Insalata di Spaghettini e Melone

Serves 4 to 6

The first time I demonstrated this recipe to a class of professional-chefs-to-be at Peter Kump's New York Cooking School, it was easy to see their skepticism. Melon and pasta did not sound promising. Once my students tasted it, however, they were quickly convinced how good it is.

The idea comes from Le Tre Vaselle, an excellent restaurant in Torgiano, between Perugia and Assisi. The restaurant, which is also a luxurious inn, is owned by the Lungarotti family of wine makers.

This salad tastes best when just made. Do not make it up more than two hours in advance of serving.

8 ounces spaghettini
Salt
5 tablespoons extra-virgin olive oil
1 cup finely chopped ripe cantaloupe
2 ounces prosciutto, coarsely chopped (about ½ cup)
¼ cup finely chopped flat-leaf parsley
¼ cup finely chopped fresh mint
2 tablespoons fresh lemon juice
Freshly ground black pepper

1. In a large pot, bring 4 quarts of water to a boil over high heat. Add the spaghettini and a generous amount of salt. Cook, stirring occasionally, until the pasta is *al dente*, tender yet still firm to the bite.

2. Pour 3 tablespoons of the olive oil into a large bowl. Drain the pasta and toss immediately with the olive oil. Let cool completely, tossing occasionally.

3. Just before serving, add the cantaloupe, prosciutto, parsley, and mint. In a small bowl, whisk together the remaining 2 tablespoons oil and the lemon juice with salt and pepper to taste. Pour over the spaghettini and toss well.

CRISP POLENTA CROSTINI

Crostini di Polenta

Serves 8

Crostini can be made with slices of polenta or bread. Grilled or fried, the polenta becomes crisp on the outside and creamy within, a perfect foil for a tasty topping.

Preparing polenta can be a bit tricky since the cornmeal has a tendency to form lumps if it is added too quickly to boiling water and it usually requires constant stirring. This double-boiler method simplifies the process and makes constant stirring unnecessary.

The polenta base can be made several days in advance and crisped just before serving. The slices can be toasted on a grill or fried in a skillet. Serve with the black olive paste (for Olive Crostini, page 145) or any topping that follows.

3 cups cold water
1 cup yellow cornmeal
1 teaspoon salt
Extra-virgin olive oil

1. In the top half of a double boiler set directly over medium heat, bring 2 cups of the water to a boil.

2. In a small bowl, combine the cornmeal and remaining 1 cup water. Stir the cornmeal mixture and salt into the boiling water. Stir constantly with a wooden spoon until the mixture comes to a boil. Place the top half of the double boiler over the bottom half partially filled with boiling water. Cover and cook, stirring occasionally, for 30 minutes, or until the polenta is thick.

3. Line a 9- × 5-inch loaf pan with plastic wrap. Pour in the polenta and let cool. Cover and refrigerate overnight or up to 3 days.

4. Brush a large baking sheet with olive oil. Preheat the broiler.

5. Invert the polenta onto a cutting board and remove the plastic wrap. Cut the polenta into ½-inch-thick slices. Arrange the slices on the baking sheet and brush the tops with olive oil.

6. Broil about 3 inches from the heat for 5 minutes on each side, or until lightly browned.

GORGONZOLA CROSTINI

Crostini di Gorgonzola

Serves 8

Mascarpone is a fresh, delicate cheese that tastes like a cross between sour cream and whipped butter. It is usually sold in plastic tubs. If possible, ask for a taste before buying. If it has a pronounced sour tang, the cheese is old. You can substitute ricotta or whipped cream cheese if mascarpone is not available.

4 ounces imported Italian Gorgonzola
¼ cup mascarpone
8 Crisp Polenta Crostini (see page 195)
2 tablespoons chopped toasted walnuts

1. Preheat the broiler.
2. In a small bowl, mash together the Gorgonzola and mascarpone. Spread each slice of polenta with 2 tablespoons of the cheese mixture.
3. Broil the crostini until the cheese is bubbling, about 2 minutes. Sprinkle with the walnuts and serve hot.

FRIED POLENTA

Polenta Fritta

Serves 10 to 12

The picturesque Antica Locanda Mincio is perched on the bank of the River Mincio at the point where the rushing river spills over a tiny waterfall in the town of Valeggio near Verona. In the warmer months, diners can eat regional specialties such as pumpkin tortellini on the shady terrace. Our meal began with a luscious antipasto of coarse, homemade salami served with crusty squares of fried polenta topped with a dab of garlic-and-parsley–scented lard.

The rich, pure corn flavor is so satisfying that fried polenta scarcely needs a topping. Serve it plain or with *salumi* (see page 238).

1 recipe Crisp Polenta Crostini (see page 195), prepared through step 3
Corn oil for frying

1. Invert the polenta onto a cutting board and remove the plastic wrap. With a thin-bladed knife, cut the polenta into slices about ⅓ inch thick. Pat the slices dry with paper towels.
2. In a deep heavy saucepan, heat about 1 inch of oil until the temperature reaches 375°F on a deep-frying thermometer.
3. Add the polenta a few pieces at a time. Fry until golden on both sides, turning once, about 8 minutes. Drain on paper towels. Serve hot.

PORCINI MUSHROOM SAUCE

Salsa di Funghi Porcini

Makes 8 servings

In Northern Italy, fat, flavorful porcini mushrooms are often served instead of meat. Dried porcini have a deep woodsy flavor even more intense than the fresh though they lack the meaty texture.

In this sauce, dried porcini are combined with cultivated mushrooms to create a semblance of fresh porcini. Serve this sauce on Crisp Polenta Crostini (page 195) or on fresh pasta.

1 ounce dried porcini mushrooms

2 cups hot water

1 large onion, peeled and finely chopped

⅓ cup extra-virgin olive oil

1 garlic clove, peeled and finely chopped

12 ounces white mushrooms, thinly sliced

1 cup drained and chopped canned peeled Italian tomatoes

½ cup dry red wine

2 tablespoons chopped flat-leaf parsley

Salt and freshly ground black pepper

1. In a small bowl, soak the porcini mushrooms in the hot water until softened, about 30 minutes.

2. Remove the mushrooms from the water, reserving the liquid. Strain the soaking liquid through a paper coffee filter or a double thickness of dampened cheesecloth and set aside. Rinse the mushrooms several times in cold water until no traces of sand remain. Finely chop the mushrooms.

3. In a large skillet, cook the onion in the olive oil over medium heat until tender, about 5 minutes.

4. Stir in the soaked mushrooms and the garlic. Add the fresh mushrooms and increase the heat to medium high. Cook for 5 minutes, stirring frequently, until the mushrooms are tender.

5. Stir in the tomatoes, wine, reserved mushroom liquid, parsley, and salt and pepper to taste. Reduce the heat to low and simmer for 10 to 15 minutes, until the sauce is thickened.

SHELLFISH AND FISH

F r u t t i   d i   M a r e   e   P e s c e

Il pesce va cucinato appena pescato.

Fish should be cooked as soon as it is caught.

Since Italy is surrounded by three different seas, some of the finest antipasti are made with seafood. The Italians have an incredible variety of fish and shellfish available to them. Dozens of types of shrimp, squid, clams, mussels, and fish are found in every market, plus many more varieties that are only available in small quantity and never leave their home port.

I once asked the padrone of a small trattoria on the Adriatic coast the name of the curious-looking seafood he had just served me. He looked thoughtful for a moment and then told me its name. "But," he added, "that is its name in our local dialect. I don't know what it is called in Italian." And I have never been able to to find out, nor have I ever seen it again.

Fin fish—either whole or cut into steaks or fillets—are more likely to be served as a main course, though small marinated fish like fresh trout, anchovies, and sardines are popular. Shellfish appear very frequently as antipasti, either raw, in warm and cold salads, stuffed, grilled, or baked.

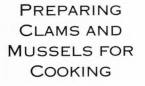

PREPARING CLAMS AND MUSSELS FOR COOKING

Cultivated mussels or clams usually are quite clean when you buy them but the "wild" varieties need to be soaked and scrubbed thoroughly to eliminate sand.

Store mussels or clams on a rack in a shallow pan set over ice in the refrigerator until ready to cook. Do not allow them to sit in liquid or they may die. Cover them with a damp towel.

When ready to use, place the mussels or clams in a large basin with cold salted water to cover. Let them soak for 15 minutes—no longer. Remove them one at a time and scrub with a stiff vegetable brush. Mussels sometimes have barnacles that can be

STUFFED CLAMS

Vongole Oreganata

Serves 4 to 6

A light dusting of crisp, garlicky bread crumbs is lovely over briny clams and a far cry from the dried-out, overcooked versions offered by some restaurants. Mussels or shrimp are also good prepared this way, or you can sprinkle the topping over scallops or fish fillets.

According to Carlo Middione, in his wonderful book *The Food of Southern Italy*, the term *oreganata* is a corruption of *ragonati*, meaning "gratinéed."

24 littleneck or other small clams
1 small garlic clove, peeled and finely chopped
¼ cup dry bread crumbs
2 tablespoons freshly grated Parmigiano-Reggiano
2 tablespoons finely chopped flat-leaf parsley
¼ cup extra-virgin olive oil
Freshly ground black pepper
Lemon wedges

1. With a stiff brush, scrub the clams well under cold running water. Place the clams and ½ cup water in a large pot. Cover and cook over high heat just until the clams open, about 5 minutes. Remove the clams as they open. Be careful not to overcook them or they will become tough. Discard any clams that do not open.

2. Twist off and discard the top half of each shell. Scrape the clam meat into a small bowl and pour the juice into another bowl. Arrange the bottom halves of the shells in a shallow baking pan.

3. If the clams are sandy, swish them one at a time in the juice, then place them in the shells. If you are using aquacultured clams, which are usually sand-free, just place the clams in the shells. Strain the clam juice through a strainer lined with dampened cheesecloth or a paper towel. Drizzle a teaspoon of the juice over each clam.

4. Preheat the broiler.

5. In a bowl, combine the garlic, bread crumbs, cheese, parsley, 2 tablespoons of the oil, and pepper to taste. Spoon some of the crumb mixture over each clam. Drizzle with the remaining 2 tablespoons olive oil.

6. Broil the clams until the crumbs are lightly browned, about 4 minutes. Serve hot with the lemon wedges.

Clams Casino Clams Casino is probably an Italian-American invention, but it is a good idea. Prepare the stuffed clams as directed through step 5. Top each with a ½-inch piece of bacon, and broil as directed until the bacon is crisp.

scraped off with a small knife. Remove the beards by pulling them toward the narrow end of the mussels.

Mussels and clams need to "breathe" and open and close their shells naturally. Discard any that do not close when tapped or any that have cracked or broken shells.

If the shellfish still seem sandy, repeat the soaking and scrubbing.

CLAMS WITH TOMATOES AND CAPERS

Vongole con Pomodori e Capperi

Serves 2 to 4

If you can find them, tiny farm-raised Manila clams from the Pacific Northwest are wonderful in this recipe. They have a sweet flavor and crunchy texture very much like the Italian *vongole*.

1 garlic clove, peeled and finely chopped
2 tablespoons chopped flat-leaf parsley
¼ cup extra-virgin olive oil
2 large ripe tomatoes, peeled, seeded, and chopped
2 tablespoons drained capers, chopped
Freshly ground black pepper
½ cup dry white wine
24 littleneck or other small clams (see page 200), soaked and scrubbed

1. In a large pot, cook the garlic and parsley in the oil over medium heat until the garlic is fragrant, about 1 minute.

2. Add the tomatoes, capers, pepper to taste, and wine. Reduce the heat to low and cook for 10 minutes.

3. Add the clams. Cover and cook just until the clams open, about 5 minutes. Remove the clams as they open. Discard any that refuse to open.

4. Pour the clams and sauce into a bowl. Serve warm or at room temperature.

MUSSELS BAKED WITH PROSCIUTTO

Cozze al Forno con Prosciutto

Serves 6 to 8

Mussels used to be full of sand and deep-sea debris, making cleaning them a real chore. Farm-raised mussels have changed all that and now the glossy black shellfish require only a minimum of attention before cooking. Just be careful not to overcook them.

2 pounds mussels, scrubbed and debearded (see page 200)
2 medium ripe tomatoes, seeded and finely chopped
¼ cup finely chopped prosciutto
2 tablespoons finely chopped flat-leaf parsley
1 garlic clove, peeled and finely chopped
Pinch of ground red pepper
About 2 tablespoons fine dry bread crumbs
2 tablespoons extra-virgin olive oil

1. Place the mussels in a large pot. Cover and cook over medium-high heat until the mussels begin to open, shaking the pan occasionally, about 4 minutes; as they open, transfer the mussels to a bowl. Continue cooking the unopened mussels a few minutes longer, then discard any that refuse to open.

2. Preheat the oven to 400°F.

3. In a small bowl, combine the tomatoes, prosciutto, parsley, garlic, and red pepper.

4. Twist off the top half of the shell from each mussel, leaving the meat in the lower half. Place the mussels on a rack in a large baking pan. Spoon a teaspoon of the tomato mixture onto each mussel. Top each with a pinch of bread crumbs and drizzle with the oil. Bake for 5 minutes, or until heated through. Serve immediately.

MUSSELS STUFFED WITH RICE

Cozze Ripiene di Riso

Serves 6 to 8

Arborio rice is the short-grain rice most frequently used to make risotto. Here it absorbs the delicious mussel juices and becomes a moist and creamy stuffing flecked with peas, scallions, and parsley.

2 pounds mussels, scrubbed and debearded (see page 200)
1 cup dry white wine
¼ cup extra-virgin olive oil
1 medium onion, peeled and finely chopped
½ cup Arborio or other short-grain rice
½ cup tiny peas, fresh or frozen
¼ teaspoon salt
⅛ teaspoon freshly ground black pepper
2 scallions, finely chopped
2 tablespoons chopped flat-leaf parsley

1. In a large pot, combine the mussels and wine. Cover and cook over medium-high heat until the mussels begin to open, shaking the pan occasionally, about 4 minutes; as the mussels open, transfer them to a bowl. Continue cooking the remaining mussels a few minutes longer, then discard any that refuse to open.

2. Pour the mussel juices into a measuring cup, add enough water to make 1¼ cups of liquid, and set aside. Remove the mussels from the shells. Twist off and discard the top halves of the shells and reserve the bottoms.

3. In a large saucepan, heat the oil over medium-low heat. Add the onion and sauté for 10 minutes, or until very tender but not browned. Add the rice. Cook, stirring constantly, for 1 minute.

4. Add the reserved liquid and bring to a simmer. Stir in the peas, salt, and pepper. Reduce the heat to low. Cover and cook for 15 to 20 minutes, or until the rice is tender.

5. Remove from the heat, and stir in the scallions, parsley, and mussels. When cool enough to handle, use a spoon to pack the rice mixture into the shells, including a mussel in each one. Serve warm or at room temperature.

MUSSELS IN WHITE WINE

Cozze al Vino Bianco

Serves 2 to 4

I serve these mussels in thick white china bowls, a stunning contrast to the blue-black shells, with spoons and lots of good bread to get all of the intensely flavored juices.

4 cloves garlic, peeled and finely chopped
½ teaspoon crushed red pepper
⅓ cup finely chopped flat-leaf parsley
3 sprigs fresh thyme or ½ teaspoon dried
⅓ cup extra-virgin olive oil
½ cup dry white wine
2 pounds mussels, scrubbed and debearded (see page 200)

1. In a large pot, cook the garlic, red pepper, parsley, and thyme in the oil over medium heat until the garlic is fragrant, about 1 minute. Add the wine and mussels. Cover and cook for 4 to 5 minutes, shaking the pan occasionally. As the mussels open, remove them from the pan with a slotted spoon and place in serving bowls. Continue cooking the unopened mussels a few minutes longer, then discard any that do not open.

2. Pour the pan juices over the mussels. Serve warm or at room temperature.

BAKED MUSSELS WITH PEPPER AND TOMATOES

Cozze Gratinate al Peperone

Serves 4 to 6

2 pounds mussels, scrubbed and debearded (see page 200)
5 to 6 tablespoons extra-virgin olive oil
1 large red bell pepper, cored, seeded, and finely chopped
1 small onion, peeled and finely chopped
2 large ripe tomatoes, peeled, seeded, and chopped
1 large garlic clove, peeled and finely chopped
Salt and freshly ground black pepper
1 tablespoon bread crumbs
1 tablespoon finely chopped flat-leaf parsley

1. Place the mussels in a large pot. Cover and cook over medium-high heat until the mussels begin to open, shaking the pot occasionally, about 4 minutes; as they open, transfer the mussels to a bowl. Continue cooking the remaining mussels a few minutes longer, then discard any that refuse to open.

2. Preheat the oven to 450°F.

3. In a large skillet, heat 4 tablespoons olive oil over medium heat. Add the pepper and cook, stirring, for about 5 minutes. Add the onion and cook for 5 minutes more. Stir in the tomatoes, garlic, and salt and pepper to taste and cook until thickened, about 5 minutes.

4. Twist off and discard the top shell of each mussel, leaving the meat in the lower half. Place the mussels on a rack in a large baking pan. Spoon about a teaspoon of the sauce over each mussel.

5. In a small bowl, combine the bread crumbs and parsley. Sprinkle over the mussels. Drizzle each with a few drops of olive oil.

6. Bake the mussels until the crumbs are lightly browned, about 10 minutes. Serve hot.

MUSSELS WITH CAPER MAYONNAISE

Cozze con Capperi

Serves 6 to 8

It is worth making homemade mayonnaise for these cold mussels. But, if that is not possible, add a couple of tablespoons of extra-virgin olive oil along with the garlic, parsley, and capers to prepared mayonnaise for a bit of homemade flavor.

2 pounds mussels, scrubbed and debearded (see page 200)
¼ cup dry white wine
1 bay leaf
½ cup mayonnaise, preferably Olive Oil Mayonnaise (see page 241)
¼ cup drained capers, finely chopped
2 tablespoons finely chopped flat-leaf parsley
1 teaspoon finely chopped garlic

1. Put the mussels in a large pot with the wine and bay leaf. Cover and place over medium heat. Cook, shaking the pot occasionally, until the mussels begin to open, about 4 minutes; as they open, transfer the mussels to a bowl. Continue cooking the unopened mussels a few minutes longer, then discard any that refuse to open.
2. In a small bowl, combine the mayonnaise, capers, parsley, and garlic.
3. Twist off and discard the top shells of each mussel, leaving the meat in the lower half. Place the mussels on a serving plate. Coat each one with some of the mayonnaise mixture. Serve immediately.

OCTOPUS AND POTATO SALAD

Insalata di Polipo e
Patate

Serves 6

Sandro Landini is a wine maker who longs for the sea. When he is not hard at work among the grapevines or making Chianti Classico and other fine red wines in the cellars of Fattoria Viticcio, his family's Tuscan estate, he is likely to be found fishing in the sapphire blue waters around Elba, an island not far from the Tuscan coast.

On a recent visit to Elba, I learned something new about octopus from Sandro. Traditional octopus-cooking lore requires that the creature be dashed against the sides of the kitchen sink before cooking in order to tenderize it. The octopus would then be dipped three or four times into boiling water to "frighten" it into submission, then simmered until done.

But Sandro, who knows all about fish, tells me that since most octopus is now sold frozen, these procedures are no longer necessary. It seems that freezing helps to break down the tough fibers and tenderizes the octopus, making it ready to cook.

1 octopus, about 3 pounds
1 bay leaf
Salt
1 pound small red potatoes
¼ cup extra-virgin olive oil
2 tablespoons red wine vinegar
1 garlic clove, peeled and finely chopped
¼ teaspoon crushed red pepper
Freshly ground black pepper
2 tablespoons chopped flat-leaf parsley

1. If the octopus is frozen, thaw it in a large bowl of cold water, changing the water frequently. Rinse the octopus well under cold running water. Remove the hard "beak" at the base of the tentacles.

2. Bring a large pot of water to a boil. Add the octopus, bay leaf, and salt to taste. Partially cover the pot and cook the octopus until tender when pierced with a fork, about 45 minutes to 1 hour (the cooking time may vary considerably).

3. Meanwhile, place the potatoes in a medium saucepan and add cold water to cover and salt to taste. Cover and bring to a simmer over medium heat. Cook until tender when pierced with a knife, about 20 minutes.

4. Drain the octopus and scrape away any loose skin with a small knife. Cut the octopus into bite-size pieces. Drain the potatoes and cut into ¼-inch slices.

5. In a large bowl, whisk together the oil, vinegar, garlic, and red pepper. Add the octopus and potatoes and toss well. Season to taste with salt and black pepper. Sprinkle with the parsley. Serve warm or at room temperature.

SKEWERED SCALLOPS WITH LEMON AND HERBS

Canestrelli in Salmoriglio

Serves 6 to 8

Salmoriglio is the classic Sicilian sauce/marinade for fish or seafood. Here it makes a lovely, light dressing for large sea scallops but other shellfish or chunks of firm-fleshed fish could be substituted.

1 pound sea scallops
Fresh or dried bay leaves
1 small mild onion, cut into 1-inch chunks and separated into layers
3 tablespoons extra-virgin olive oil
1½ tablespoons fresh lemon juice
½ teaspoon dried oregano
Salt and freshly ground black pepper

1. Preheat the grill or broiler.
2. On 8 short skewers, thread the scallops alternately with bay leaves and the pieces of onion.
3. In a small bowl, whisk together the oil, lemon juice, oregano, and salt and pepper to taste. Brush the scallops with some of the sauce.
4. Grill or broil until the scallops are just opaque, about 3 to 4 minutes on each side. Place the skewers on a serving plate and drizzle with the remaining sauce.

WARM SHRIMP AND GREEN BEAN SALAD

Insalata Calda di Gamberi e Fagiolini

Serves 4 to 6

At the Taverna del Pittore in Arona on Lake Maggiore you can arrive in your speedboat and enjoy this pretty salad on the restaurant's sunny lakeside terrace.

¼ **cup extra-virgin olive oil**
1 **tablespoon fresh lemon juice**
¼ **cup snipped fresh chives**
Salt and freshly ground black pepper
1 **pound tender green beans, trimmed**
1 **pound medium shrimp, shelled and deveined**
Lemon slices

1. In a small bowl, whisk together the olive oil, lemon juice, chives, and salt and pepper to taste until well blended.

2. Bring a large saucepan of water to a boil. Add the green beans and salt to taste. Cook until the beans are tender, about 5 minutes. Drain well. Place the beans on a platter and toss with half of the dressing.

3. In the same saucepan, bring 2 quarts of water to a boil. Add the shrimp and salt to taste. Cook just until the shrimp are opaque, about 2 minutes. Drain well and place them in a small bowl with the remaining dressing. Let marinate for 5 minutes, stirring occasionally.

4. Spoon the shrimp over the green beans. Garnish with the lemon slices.

SHRIMP WITH FENNEL AND OLIVES

Gamberi con Finocchio e Olive

Serves 6 to 8

These shrimp can be marinated overnight in the refrigerator, but let them come to room temperature before serving.

1½ pounds medium shrimp
Salt
2 garlic cloves, peeled
1 tablespoon fennel seeds
⅓ cup extra-virgin olive oil
¼ cup fresh lemon juice
Freshly ground black pepper
½ cup Kalamata or other imported black olives

1. Bring a medium saucepan of water to a boil. Add the shrimp and salt to taste. Cook just until opaque, about 2 minutes. Drain the shrimp. Peel and devein them.
2. Lightly crush the garlic cloves with the side of a heavy knife. Crush the fennel seeds the same way.
3. In a medium bowl, whisk together the oil, lemon juice, garlic, and fennel with salt and pepper to taste. Add the shrimp and olives and mix well. Let marinate for at least 1 hour, stirring occasionally. Remove the garlic before serving.

MARINATED SHRIMP AND MUSHROOMS

Marinata di Gamberi e Funghi

Serves 6

1 pound small white mushrooms, trimmed
¼ cup white wine vinegar
Salt
1 pound medium shrimp, peeled and deveined
4 anchovy fillets
1 hard-cooked egg, chopped
2 tablespoons finely chopped onion
1 large garlic clove, peeled and finely chopped
1 tablespoon drained capers
Pinch of crushed red pepper
1 tablespoon fresh lemon juice
⅓ cup extra-virgin olive oil
½ cup chopped flat-leaf parsley
Radicchio leaves

1. Bring a large pot of water to a boil. Add the mushrooms, vinegar, and salt to taste. Cook for 5 minutes. Add the shrimp and cook just until opaque, about 2 minutes. Pour into a strainer and cool under cold running water. Drain well.

2. In a medium bowl, mash the anchovies with a wooden spoon. Add the egg, onion, garlic, capers, and red pepper. Stir in the lemon juice. With a wire whisk, gradually beat in the olive oil.

3. In a serving bowl, combine the mushrooms and shrimp, parsley, and dressing and stir well. Chill for 1 to 2 hours before serving. Serve on radicchio leaves.

PRAWN AND BEAN SALAD

Scampi con Fagioli

Serves 4

The first time I tasted this salad it was prepared with delicately flavored freshwater prawns. The prawns, which are farm-raised, are sold fresh, never frozen. They resemble tiny lobsters with long thin claws and are bluish-gray when raw but turn a creamy coral color when cooked. Large shrimp can be substituted.

1 celery rib, coarsely chopped

1 carrot, coarsely chopped

1 medium onion, peeled

1 leek, trimmed and halved lengthwise

1 slice lemon

12 freshwater prawns or 1¼ pounds large shrimp

2½ cups warm drained cooked cannellini beans (see page 74) or 1 19-ounce can cannellini beans, rinsed and drained

¼ cup extra-virgin olive oil plus additional for serving

2 medium tomatoes, peeled, seeded, and diced

¼ cup chopped fresh basil plus 4 whole leaves

Salt and freshly ground black pepper

1. In a large pot, combine the celery, carrot, onion, leek, lemon, and 6 cups water. Bring to a simmer and cook for 30 minutes.

2. Add the prawns or shrimp and cook for 3 to 4 minutes, or until just cooked through. Remove the prawns or shrimp from the pot and discard the cooking liquid and vegetables. Twist the heads off the prawns and reserve 4 of them for garnish; peel the tails. If using shrimp, peel and devein them.

3. In a large bowl, combine the warm beans, ¼ cup oil, tomatoes, chopped basil, and salt and pepper to taste. Gently stir in the prawn tails or the shrimp. Spoon onto four serving plates. Garnish each with a prawn head and a basil leaf and drizzle with a few drops of olive oil. Serve immediately.

SHRIMP AND ZUCCHINI SALAD WITH MINT

Insalata di Gamberi alla Menta

Serves 4 to 6

Cooking the shrimp and zucchini in a vegetable-flavored broth adds extra flavor. This lovely, light salad is best when it is freshly made.

1 small onion, peeled
1 rib celery
1 medium carrot
1 pound small zucchini, scrubbed
Salt
1 pound large shrimp
2 medium tomatoes, peeled, seeded, and diced
¼ cup chopped fresh mint
½ cup extra-virgin olive oil
2 to 3 tablespoons fresh lemon juice
1 tablespoon balsamic vinegar
Freshly ground black pepper

1. In a large saucepan, combine the onion, celery, carrot, and 2 quarts water. Bring to a simmer and cook for 30 minutes.
2. Add the zucchini and salt to taste. Cook until the zucchini is crisp-tender, about 8 minutes. Remove the zucchini from the pot and drain on paper towels.
3. Add the shrimp to the pot. Cook just until opaque, about 3 minutes. Drain and cool the shrimp under cold running water. Discard the cooking liquid and vegetables. Peel and devein the shrimp.
4. Cut the zucchini into 2- × ¼- × ¼-inch strips and arrange them on a platter. Spoon the shrimp and tomatoes over the zucchini.
5. In a small bowl, whisk together the mint, olive oil, lemon juice, vinegar, and salt and pepper to taste until well blended. Drizzle over the shrimp and vegetables. Serve immediately.

215

BUTTERFLIED SHRIMP IN GARLIC AND ANCHOVY SAUCE

Gamberoni con Aglio e Acciughe

Serves 4 to 6

In a little trattoria in Santa Maria Ligure, we ate big red shrimp bathed in a sensational sauce of garlic and anchovies, followed by steaming bowls of spaghetti with fresh tomatoes and *triglie* (red mullet). Needless to say, we all but licked our plates clean.

1 pound jumbo shrimp
⅓ cup extra-virgin olive oil
1 tablespoon finely chopped garlic
4 to 6 anchovy fillets (according to taste), finely chopped
½ cup dry white wine
2 tablespoons fresh lemon juice
Salt and freshly ground black pepper
Chopped flat-leaf parsley

1. Peel the shrimp, leaving the tail sections intact. With a small knife, butterfly the shrimp by making a deep cut lengthwise down the back of each one. Remove the dark vein, if any. Open the shrimp flat like a book.

2. Preheat the broiler. In a large skillet with a flameproof handle, heat the olive oil, garlic, and anchovies over medium heat. Cook, stirring, until the garlic is fragrant, about 1 minute. Add the wine and lemon juice and cook for 1 minute more. Remove from the heat.

3. Place the shrimp in the skillet cut side down. Sprinkle the shrimp with a pinch of salt and a grind or two of pepper and baste with the sauce.

4. Broil the shrimp about 4 inches from the heat just until opaque, about 3 minutes. Sprinkle with the parsley and serve warm.

LARGE SHRIMP WITH CELERY, RAISINS AND CINNAMON

Gamberoni in Dolceforte

Serves 4 to 6

This dish dates back to the Renaissance, when it was made with crayfish from the Arno River in Florence. The name *dolceforte* usually indicates foods that are sweet and hot, though in this case cinnamon is used instead of hot pepper. The combination of shrimp, raisins, celery, and spice is intriguing, just the kind of thing I imagine the Medicis would have eaten.

4 tender celery ribs, trimmed and cut into 2- × ¼- × ¼-inch strips

2 tablespoons unsalted butter

1 teaspoon sugar

Salt

Freshly ground black pepper

3 tablespoons extra-virgin olive oil

1 pound large shrimp, peeled and deveined

¼ teaspoon ground cinnamon

⅓ cup dry white wine

2 tablespoons fresh lemon juice

¼ cup golden raisins

1. In a medium saucepan, combine the celery, butter, sugar, ¼ teaspoon salt, and pepper to taste. Add ¼ cup water and cook over medium-low heat until the celery is tender and most of the liquid has evaporated, about 10 minutes.

2. Meanwhile, in a medium skillet, heat the olive oil over medium-high heat. Add the shrimp and cook, turning once, until lightly browned, about 1 minute on each side. Sprinkle with the cinnamon and salt and pepper to taste. Add the wine, lemon juice, and raisins. Cook for 2 minutes more.

3. Arrange the shrimp and raisins on a platter and spoon on the celery. Serve hot.

Though squid are often said to be sold cleaned, it is rare to find a fish market that does a really thorough job of it, so you're better off starting from scratch.

Hold the body of the squid in one hand and the head and tentacles in the other. Gently pull the two apart. Cut off the tentacles just above the eyes. Discard the lower portion. Squeeze the base of the tentacles to extract the hard, round "beak."

Squeeze the viscera out of the body and pull out the long plasticlike quill. Rinse the inside of the body sac thoroughly to eliminate sand. Removing the skin is optional. To do so, pull off the purplish covering with your fingers.

SKEWERED GRILLED SHRIMP AND SQUID

Spiedini di Scampi e Calamari

Serves 4

A light coating of garlicky crumbs keeps the delicate seafood from drying out under the intense heat of the broiler or grill.

8 ounces medium shrimp, peeled and deveined
8 ounces cleaned squid (see at left), cut into ¾-inch rings
½ cup dry bread crumbs
2 tablespoons finely chopped flat-leaf parsley
1 small garlic clove, peeled and finely chopped
Salt and freshly ground black pepper
3 tablespoons extra-virgin olive oil
Lemon wedges

1. Preheat the broiler or prepare a medium-hot fire in a barbecue grill.
2. In a bowl, combine all the ingredients except the lemon wedges. Stir to coat the shrimp and squid. Thread the shrimp and pieces of squid alternately onto skewers.
3. Grill or broil until the shrimp and squid are lightly browned, about 3 minutes on each side. Serve hot with the lemon wedges.

GRILLED SQUID

Creste di Calamari

Serves 4

To prevent large squid from curling up on a hot grill, slits are cut into their body sacs. When the squid are cooked, the slits open and resemble a rooster's crest. After grilling, the squid are lightly dressed with a flavorful sauce spiked with garlic and oregano.

Be careful not to overcook squid or they will toughen.

8 large squid, cleaned (see page 218)
¼ cup extra-virgin olive oil
2 tablespoons dry white wine
1 tablespoon fresh lemon juice
1 small garlic clove, peeled and minced
½ teaspoon dried oregano
Salt and freshly ground black pepper
1 tablespoon finely chopped flat-leaf parsley

1. To form "crests," make crosswise slits ½ inch apart in the body sacs of the squid without cutting them all the way through. Grilling the tentacles is optional. If you do grill them, it is a good idea to use a fine-mesh grill rack to prevent them from slipping into the flames.

2. In a shallow dish, combine the squid, 2 tablespoons of the oil, and the wine. Marinate for 1 hour. Prepare a medium-hot fire in a barbecue grill or preheat a broiler.

3. In a shallow serving dish, whisk together the remaining olive oil, the wine, lemon juice, garlic, oregano, and salt and pepper to taste.

4. Remove the squid from the marinade and pat dry. Grill or broil, turning once, until opaque and lightly browned, about 4 minutes. Place them in a shallow dish and drizzle with the dressing. Sprinkle with the parsley. Serve warm or at room temperature.

Undercooked or overcooked squid can be tough. When grilling, poaching, or frying, cook squid just until it is opaque, about 1 minute. When cooked in a sauce, squid will need longer cooking and will first toughen, then become tender after 20 minutes or so of simmering.

SEAFOOD SALAD
WITH PESTO

Insalata di Mare al
Pesto

Serves 4 to 6

This salad is inspired by one served at the Locanda da Angelo, a restaurant and inn in Ameglia, near Pisa. Angelo Paracucchi is a renowned chef, one reason being that he appreciates the importance of his raw materials and knows how to make the most of them.

One day I asked him what made a certain seafood salad, which seemed to contain only a few varieties of tiny warm fish and shellfish bathed in olive oil, so extraordinarily good. Signor Paracucchi took no credit and replied that the secret was the freshness of the fish—they were less than three hours out of the water.

It is not easy to get seafood as fresh as that, unless, of course, you catch the fish yourself, but buy the freshest seafood possible.

Pesto

1 small bunch basil
½ bunch flat-leaf parsley
1 small garlic clove, peeled
2 tablespoons toasted pine nuts
⅓ cup extra-virgin olive oil
½ teaspoon salt

4 medium red potatoes (about 12 ounces), cut into ¼-inch slices
½ pound green beans
Salt
¼ cup extra-virgin olive oil
2 tablespoons fresh lemon juice

¼ **pound medium shrimp, peeled and deveined**
½ **pound bay scallops**
1 **pound cleaned squid (see page 218), cut into**
  ½ **-inch rings**
1 **tablespoon toasted pine nuts**

1. To make the pesto, rinse the basil and parsley and remove the leaves from the stems. Dry well with paper towels. You should have about 1 cup basil leaves and ½ cup parsley leaves.

2. In a food processor or blender, coarsely chop the basil and parsley. Add the garlic and pine nuts and chop fine. With the machine running, slowly add the olive oil. Add the salt. Set aside.

3. Place the potatoes in a medium saucepan and add cold water to cover and salt to taste. Bring to a simmer and cook over low heat until tender, about 5 minutes. Drain.

4. Meanwhile, bring another medium saucepan of water to a boil. Add the green beans and salt to taste. Cook, uncovered, over medium heat until the beans are crisp-tender, about 5 minutes. Drain and rinse under cold running water. Pat dry.

5. In a large bowl, whisk together the olive oil, lemon juice, and a pinch of salt. Set aside.

6. Bring a large pot of salted water to a boil. Add the shrimp and cook for 1 minute. Add the scallops and cook for 1 minute more. Add the squid and cook for 1 minute more or until all the shellfish are opaque. Drain well.

7. Add the shellfish to the dressing and toss well. Arrange the potato slices on a large serving plate. Top with the green beans. Spoon the shellfish and their dressing over the vegetables and top with the pesto. Sprinkle with the pine nuts and serve immediately.

FRIED SQUID

Calamari Fritti

Serves 6 to 8

Fried squid have become a popular appetizer in many restaurants. Though some cooks use heavy batters to coat the squid, this is the authentic Italian way. Properly done, these squid are crunchy and golden brown and not at all tough. My favorite part is the delicious curly tentacles.

Peeled shrimp or zucchini sticks can also be fried this way.

2 pounds cleaned squid (see page 218)
1 cup all-purpose flour
1 teaspoon salt
Freshly ground black pepper
Vegetable oil for frying
Lemon wedges

1. Cut the squid sacs into ½-inch rings. Cut the tentacles in half through the base. Dry on paper towels.

2. On a piece of wax paper, combine the flour, salt, and pepper to taste.

3. Add oil to a depth of about 2 inches into a deep heavy saucepan or fill a deep fryer with oil according to the manufacturer's recommendation. Heat the oil to 375°F on a deep-frying thermometer. When the oil has reached the correct temperature, lightly coat the squid pieces a few at a time with the flour. Shake the pieces to remove the excess flour. Carefully lower enough squid a few pieces at a time into the hot oil. Do not crowd, or the squid will not cook properly.

4. Cook until the squid turn a light golden brown, about 3 minutes. Remove the squid with a slotted spoon and drain well on paper towels. Repeat with the remaining squid. Serve hot with the lemon wedges.

SPICY SQUID SALAD

Insalata di Calamari

Serves 6 to 8

All kinds of seafood are used in salads in Italy. Squid are particularly popular since their firm, slightly chewy texture holds up well in a marinade.

2 pounds cleaned squid (see page 218)
⅓ cup extra-virgin olive oil
3 tablespoons red wine vinegar
1 garlic clove, peeled and finely chopped
½ teaspoon dried oregano
½ teaspoon salt
¼ teaspoon crushed red pepper
2 tender celery ribs, thinly sliced
½ cup sliced pitted green olives
2 tablespoons chopped flat-leaf parsley

1. Cut the squid sacs into ½-inch rings. Cut the tentacles in half through the base.
2. Bring a large saucepan of water to a boil over high heat. Add the squid and cook just until opaque, about 1 minute. Drain and rinse under cold running water.
3. In a large bowl, whisk together the oil, vinegar, garlic, oregano, salt, and red pepper. Stir in the squid, celery, olives, and parsley. Cover and chill for 1 hour or overnight.
4. Just before serving, taste and correct the seasoning.

HOT GARLIC
AND ANCHOVY DIP

Bagna Caôda

Serves 8

Bagna caôda means "hot bath" in Piemontese dialect and what a delightful bath this is. It is usually served in a chafing dish or fondue pot placed in the middle of the table. Supply long forks for spearing the vegetables and plenty of chewy bread to soak up any drips. The assortment of vegetables can be cooked and/or raw, but should reflect the season.

Leftover bagna caôda is a delicious sauce for pasta, vegetables, or boiled meats. In Piedmont, an egg is scrambled into whatever remains in the chafing dish to soak up the flavors of the sauce and vegetables.

½ cup extra-virgin olive oil

8 medium garlic cloves, peeled and finely chopped

2 2-ounce cans anchovy fillets with their liquid

4 tablespoons unsalted butter

About 8 cups assorted raw vegetables cut into spears or sliced, such as carrots, red and yellow bell peppers, Jerusalem artichokes, scallions, celery, or tender cabbage leaves and/or cooked vegetables such as peeled roasted peppers, boiled potatoes, roasted whole onions, or blanched cauliflower

Italian or peasant bread, thickly sliced

1. In a small saucepan, combine the olive oil, garlic, and anchovies with their liquid. Cook and stir over medium heat, mashing the anchovies with a wooden spoon, for about 5 minutes. Add the butter and stir just until it is melted.

2. Pour the sauce into a small chafing dish or fondue pot set over a candle or other gentle warming device. Serve immediately with the vegetables and crusty bread.

SALT COD AND OLIVE SALAD

Insalata di Baccalà

Serves 6

Baccalà is salt cod. There are two kinds, one that is salted and dried and one that is salted and refrigerated. Both need to be soaked to eliminate excess salt and soften them. The refrigerated kind is less salty and requires less time to desalt it. If it is not available, use dried baccalà and soak it for at least 24 hours.

Don't confuse baccalà with *stoccafisso* (stockfish), cod that is air-dried without being salted. However, it also could be prepared this way.

1 pound baccalà (salt cod)
2 tablespoons extra-virgin olive oil
2 celery ribs, thinly sliced
1 large onion, peeled and finely chopped
½ cup imported black olives, such as Kalamata,
  pitted and chopped
2 tablespoons white wine vinegar
1 teaspoon sugar
¼ teaspoon dried oregano
Freshly ground black pepper
2 tablespoons chopped flat-leaf parsley

1. Wash the cod under cool running water. Cut the fish into 3 or 4 pieces. Place the pieces in a bowl and cover with cool water. Refrigerate for 12 to 24 hours, changing the water 4 or 5 times.

2. In a large pot, bring about 2 inches of fresh water to a boil. Reduce the heat to low. Add the baccalà and simmer for 5 minutes, or until tender. Drain the fish and, using your fingers, carefully remove the bones. Place the fish on a large serving platter.

3. In a large skillet, heat the oil over medium heat. Add the celery, onion, and olives and cook until the onion is tender, about 5 minutes. Stir in the vinegar, sugar, and oregano. Pour the mixture over the baccalà. Sprinkle with pepper to taste and the parsley. Serve at room temperature.

SALT COD PUREE

Baccalà Mantecato

Serves 8 to 10

This recipe makes a lot, so it is great for a large party. Keep the mixture warm in a chafing dish. It also reheats well, so it can be made ahead. For best results, pass the potatoes through a ricer or food mill; a food processor will make them gummy.

Olive paste makes a delicious flavor and color contrast to the suave flavor of the fish puree, but if you prefer, you can eliminate it.

1 pound baccalà (salt cod)
1 celery rib
1 onion, peeled
½ lemon
1½ pounds boiling potatoes (about 4 medium),
 peeled and cut into quarters
1 garlic clove, peeled
Salt
½ cup extra-virgin olive oil
About ¼ cup fresh lemon juice
Freshly ground black pepper
½ cup finely chopped flat-leaf parsley
Thin slices of toasted Italian bread
Pasta d'olive (olive paste) or chopped imported
 black olives, optional

1. Wash the cod under cool running water. Cut the fish into 3 or 4 pieces. To remove as much of the salt as possible, place the fish in a bowl and cover with cool water. Refrigerate for 12 to 24 hours, changing the water 4 or 5 times.

2. In a medium saucepan, bring 2 quarts of water to a boil over high heat. Add the celery, onion, and lemon. Reduce the heat to low. Cook for 10 minutes. Add the cod and simmer for 5 minutes or just until tender. Remove the cod with a slotted spoon. Using your fingers, carefully remove the bones. Discard the cooking liquid and vegetables.

3. Place the potatoes in a medium saucepan with cold water to cover. Add the garlic and salt to taste. Cover and bring to a simmer over medium heat. Reduce the heat to low and cook until the potatoes are tender, about 20 minutes. Drain, reserving the cooking water. Mash the potatoes and garlic in a food mill or pass them through a ricer into a large bowl.

4. Puree the cod in a food mill or processor. Stir the cod into the mashed potatoes. With a whisk, beat in the oil and lemon juice. The mixture should be of a spreadable consistency; if it is too thick, stir in some of the reserved potato water. Taste for seasoning and add salt, pepper, or lemon juice if desired. Stir in the parsley.

5. Serve warm with the toasted bread. Top each portion with a dollop of olive paste if desired.

SMOKED SALMON WITH FENNEL

Salmone con Finocchio

Serves 4

As delicious as it is, smoked salmon can be very rich. Here, the fresh combination of fennel and lemon cuts through the richness and the result is light and bracing. This is how Angelo Paracucchi serves it at the Locanda da Angelo in Ameglia, giving the salmon a distinctly Italian touch.

If the fennel you purchase has been trimmed of its leaves, substitute chopped parsley for the fennel tops.

1 medium bulb fennel
¼ cup extra-virgin olive oil
2 tablespoons fresh lemon juice
Salt and freshly ground black pepper
8 ounces thinly sliced smoked salmon

1. Trim off the leafy green tops of the fennel, if any. Chop fine and set aside. Slice the fennel bulb as thin as possible. There should be about 2 cups.
2. In a bowl, whisk together the olive oil, lemon juice, fennel tops (or parsley), and salt and pepper to taste. Add the sliced fennel and toss well.
3. Arrange the salmon on four plates. Spoon the fennel mixture over the salmon. Serve immediately.

TUNA, CELERY, AND BEAN SALAD

Insalata di Tonno, Sedano, e Fagioli

Serves 4

Canned Italian tuna packed in olive oil can be very fine with a tender, moist texture and rich tuna flavor. The best brands come packed in glass jars and are often available in Italian grocery stores.

Tuna, beans, and red onion are a classic combination. Here, tender celery adds a bit of crunch.

2½ cups drained cooked cranberry or cannellini beans (see page 74) or 1 19-ounce can cannellini beans, rinsed and drained
1 6½-ounce can tuna packed in olive oil, drained
2 tender celery ribs, sliced
½ small red onion, peeled and chopped
3 tablespoons extra-virgin olive oil
1 to 2 tablespoons fresh lemon juice
Freshly ground black pepper
2 tablespoons chopped flat-leaf parsley

1. In a medium bowl, combine the beans, tuna, celery, and onion.
2. In a small bowl, whisk together the olive oil, lemon juice, and pepper to taste until well blended. Drizzle over the salad. Sprinkle with the parsley and serve.

SPINACH AND TUNA ROLL

Rotolo di Spinaci e Tonno

Serves 8 to 10

Spinach, potatoes, and canned tuna come together in this simple yet elegant pâté. Served on rounds of toasted bread.

1 pound fresh spinach, washed and trimmed
Salt
1 6½-ounce can tuna packed in olive oil, drained and finely chopped
½ cup freshly grated Parmigiano-Reggiano
3 large eggs, lightly beaten
2 medium potatoes, cooked and mashed (you should have ¾ cup)
2 garlic cloves, peeled and minced
Freshly ground black pepper
⅓ cup extra-virgin olive oil
¼ cup fresh lemon juice
2 tablespoons chopped drained capers
2 tablespoons chopped flat-leaf parsley

1. Place the spinach in a large pot and sprinkle with 1 teaspoon salt. Cover and cook over medium heat until the spinach is wilted, about 5 minutes. Drain the spinach and let cool. Wrap it in a towel and squeeze out as much liquid as possible. Chop fine.

2. In a bowl, combine the spinach, tuna, Parmigiano, eggs, mashed potatoes, garlic, and salt and pepper to taste. Mix well.

3. Place an 18-inch-long piece of plastic wrap on a flat surface. Spoon the spinach mixture lengthwise down the center into a 10-inch log. Roll up the log in the plastic wrap and twist the ends. Fold the ends under. Wrap in a second piece of plastic wrap, being sure to cover the seam of the first piece. Tie the ends with kitchen twine.

4. In a pot large enough to hold the roll, bring about 4 quarts of water to a boil. Add the roll. Cover and cook for 25 minutes, turning the roll occasionally. Carefully remove the roll and let cool slightly on a rack.

5. Refrigerate until well chilled.

6. To serve, remove the plastic wrap and cut the roll into ½-inch-thick slices. Arrange the slices on a platter. In a small bowl, whisk together the oil, lemon juice, capers, parsley, and pepper to taste and drizzle over the roll.

TUNA AND VEGETABLE SALAD

Tonno con le Verdure

Serves 4 to 6

If you thought tuna salad had to include mayo and chopped celery, this one may make you reconsider. You can serve it with quartered hard-cooked eggs and some good bread for a complete meal.

1 large tomato, cut into wedges
1 small red onion, peeled and thinly sliced
1 small cucumber, peeled and sliced
1 6½-ounce can tuna packed in olive oil, drained
2 tablespoons extra-virgin olive oil
1 tablespoon fresh lemon juice
½ teaspoon dried oregano, crumbled
Freshly ground black pepper

1. In a large bowl, combine the vegetables. Break the tuna into chunks and add to the bowl.

2. In a small bowl, whisk the olive oil, lemon juice, oregano, and pepper to taste until blended. Drizzle over the salad. Toss to combine and serve.

MARINATED TROUT WITH ONIONS

Trota in Carpione

Serves 4 to 8

Many different foods can be prepared *in carpione*, "in the style of carp." Eggs, veal scallopine, zucchini, and many kinds of fish typically are fried and marinated with vinegar, onions, and herbs. Marinating mellows and marries the sharp flavors. Foods cooked *in carpione* are always served chilled.

Luciana Currado of the Vietti winery in Piedmont, an expert cook, feels that three days of marinating is just about right for trout, if you can resist eating it for that long. Luciana serves the fish with sliced garden tomatoes and a green bean salad.

4 brook trout fillets or small salmon fillets (about 1¼ pounds)
⅓ cup all-purpose flour
½ teaspoon salt
Freshly ground black pepper
¼ cup plus 2 tablespoons extra-virgin olive oil
2 large onions, peeled and thinly sliced
1 large garlic clove, peeled and finely chopped
5 fresh sage leaves or 2 teaspoons dried
Pinch of dried oregano
½ cup white wine vinegar
½ cup dry white wine

1. Rinse the fillets and pat them dry with paper towels. On a piece of wax paper, combine the flour, salt, and pepper to taste.
2. In a large skillet, heat the ¼ cup olive oil over medium heat. Dredge 2 fillets in the flour mixture and shake them to remove the excess. Place the fillets skin side up in the skillet and fry until lightly browned, about 2 minutes. Turn the fillets and fry for 1 to

2 minutes more. With a slotted spatula, transfer the fillets to a shallow glass or ceramic dish large enough to hold all of the fish in a single layer. Repeat with the remaining fillets.

3. Wipe out the skillet. Add the remaining 2 tablespoons oil and the onions and cook over medium-low heat, stirring occasionally, until very tender, about 10 minutes.

4. Stir in the garlic, sage, and oregano. Add the vinegar and wine and bring to a boil. Reduce the heat to a simmer and cook for 5 minutes.

5. Pour the mixture over the trout. Let cool slightly, then cover and refrigerate for at least 24 hours or up to 3 days before serving. Let the trout stand at room temperature to warm slightly before serving.

MEAT AND POULTRY

Carne e Pollame

Meat is not a featured player on the antipasto stage, yet it often has a starring role. Cold cured meats, known collectively as *salumi*, are frequently served as antipasti. The most familiar presentation is the classic prosciutto and melon, though there are many variations on that theme.

Apart from salumi, though, meats generally are served in small quantities, usually as a stuffing for vegetables or tossed into a salad. However, you could add a thinly sliced steak or butterflied leg of lamb to an antipasto assortment table to round out a meal.

Italian chicken salads usually include lots of vegetables for color and crunchy texture and are dressed with light, fresh olive oil–based dressings rather than mayonnaise. They are served at room temperature or lightly chilled, but never refrigerator-cold. Made in larger quantities, some of these salads are substantial enough to be served as one-dish meals.

Carne e pesce ti fanno vivere a lungo.

Meat and fish make you live a long time.

PROSCIUTTO

Prosciutto is Italian ham, and what wonderful ham it is. The slices are silky, pink, and slightly chewy. After an absence of many years, authentic prosciutto from Italy, called prosciutto di Parma, is once again available in this country. Prosciutto di Parma is exceptionally sweet, not salty, and moist, with a rich ham flavor. All other prosciutto sold here is made domestically or imported from Switzerland or Canada and the quality is variable.

When buying prosciutto, choose the kind that has been cured with its bone in for best flavor. Take a look at the cut side of the ham to see that it is fresh and not dried out. Have the meat sliced thin, but not so thin that it cannot hold its shape. The fat from

PROSCIUTTO AND GOAT CHEESE ROULADES

Involtini di Prosciutto e Caprino

Serves 8

I am always on the lookout for antipasti that require no cooking and this is one of my favorites, an idea from the splendid antipasto table at Vecchia Lugana Restaurant on Lake Garda.

The prosciutto should be thinly sliced, but not so wafer thin that the slices cannot be separated without tearing.

8 ounces mild fresh goat cheese
2 tablespoons finely chopped flat-leaf parsley
1 small garlic clove, peeled and finely chopped
**4 ounces thinly sliced prosciutto, cut into
  3-inch strips (you should have about 24 pieces)**
1 tablespoon extra-virgin olive oil
1 tablespoon fresh lemon juice
Freshly ground black pepper

1. In a bowl, beat the goat cheese, parsley, and garlic until well blended.
2. Place about 2 teaspoons on one end of each strip of prosciutto. Roll up the strips and arrange on a plate.
3. Sprinkle with the olive oil, lemon juice, and pepper to taste. Serve at room temperature.

RAW BEEF SALAD

Carpaccio

Serves 4

Giuseppe Cipriani, original owner of the famous Harry's Bar in Venice, had a problem. What should he serve to a certain contessa who had been advised by her physician to avoid eating cooked meats? Inspired by the colors in the paintings of Carpaccio, whose works were on exhibit at that time, he thinly sliced some tender raw beef and served it with a caper-and-mayonnaise—based sauce. The countess was delighted and the dish, named for the painter who inspired it, became a staple on Harry's menu.

This version of carpaccio is currently a favorite in Italy, where it is eaten as an antipasto or main course salad. When they are in season, fresh porcini mushrooms are often served instead of arugula.

Partially freezing the beef makes it easier to slice thin.

8-ounce piece Parmigiano-Reggiano, at room temperature
1 pound beef round steak or filet mignon, partially frozen
Fresh lemon juice
Salt
Freshly ground black pepper
2 bunches arugula, washed and trimmed (about 4 cups)
½ cup extra-virgin olive oil

1. With a vegetable peeler, shave the Parmigiano into thin slices.
2. Using a slicing machine or an electric knife, cut the beef into paper-thin slices. Arrange the slices, overlapping them slightly, on four chilled plates. Sprinkle with lemon juice, a pinch of salt, and pepper to taste.
3. Arrange the arugula over the beef. Drizzle each serving with 2 tablespoons of the olive oil. Scatter the cheese over the arugula. Serve immediately.

the prosciutto is very tasty and is often used in cooking. If you are fortunate enough to acquire a prosciutto bone, add it to a pot of beans or vegetable soup.

Prosciutto can be served with other meats or with tender, ripe fruits such as cantaloupe or honeydew melon, figs, pears, or persimmons. Prosciutto is also good accompanied by mostarda, the jewel-like fruits in sweet-hot mustard syrup. Or a thin slice can be wrapped around a cooked asparagus spear, small bundle of green beans, or a breadstick. Another lovely combination is prosciutto with a mild, fresh mozzarella.

An authentic Italian touch would be to serve prosciutto with bread and sweet butter, probably the only time, other than breakfast, when Italians eat butter with their bread.

SLICED CURED MEATS

Affetati Misti

Affetati misti *or sa-lumi means an assort-ment of thinly sliced cold cuts, a frequently served antipasto. The selection varies according to the region and its local specialties. A typical combination might in-clude mortadella, with or without pistachios, the luscious prototype for American-style bologna; finocchiona, the coarse-grained, fennel-flavored salami from Tuscany; bresaola, air-dried beef; and some prosciutto crudo.*

Italian salumi may be made from pork, beef, venison, wild boar, or even goose. Though many of these products are not imported here yet, real

CALF'S LIVER IN VINEGAR AND MINT

Fegato Marinato

Serves 6

When I was growing up, Easter Sunday lunch at our house always began with stuffed hard-cooked eggs and this spicy antipasto of sautéed calf's liver marinated in red wine vinegar flavored with mint and garlic. The flavorings both complement and lighten the richness of the meat.

1 pound calf's liver (about ½ inch thick)
¼ cup extra-virgin olive oil
Salt and freshly ground black pepper
3 garlic cloves, peeled and thinly sliced
¼ cup red wine vinegar
¼ cup chopped fresh mint
½ teaspoon crushed red pepper

1. Cut the liver into 2- × 1-inch pieces. Trim away the gristle and veins.
2. Heat 2 tablespoons of the oil in a large skillet over medium heat. Add the liver and cook, turning once, until browned on all sides, about 10 minutes. With a slotted spoon, transfer the liver to a shallow bowl. Sprinkle with salt and pepper to taste.
3. In a small saucepan, heat the remaining 2 tablespoons oil over medium-low heat. Add the garlic and cook for 2 to 3 minutes, until lightly golden. Add the vinegar, mint, and red pepper. Cook for 2 minutes more.
4. Pour the vinegar mixture over the liver. Let cool. Cover and refrigerate for at least several hours or overnight. Taste and adjust the seasoning. Serve slightly chilled.

CHICKEN LIVER SALAD

Insalata di Fegatini all'Aceto Balsamico

Serves 4

I love the contrast of the zesty flavors of watercress and garlic against the suaveness of the livers and balsamic vinegar in this quick salad.

4 ounces chicken livers
2 tablespoons balsamic vinegar
2 tablespoons extra-virgin olive oil
1 small garlic clove, peeled and finely chopped
Salt and freshly ground black pepper
1 tablespoon unsalted butter
2 bunches watercress, tough stems removed (about 4 cups)

1. Trim the connective tissue and bits of fat from the livers. Divide each liver in half. Rinse the livers under cold running water.
2. In a shallow serving bowl, whisk together the vinegar, oil, garlic, and salt and pepper to taste.
3. In a medium skillet, melt the butter over medium-low heat. Cook the livers until lightly browned yet still pink in the center, about 2 minutes on each side. Sprinkle lightly with salt and pepper.
4. Add the watercress to the dressing and toss. Top with the livers and serve immediately.

Italian prosciutto is now available in this country. In addition, several large American and Canadian manufacturers make good-quality Italian-style salumi, as do small butcher shops and delis in many Italian neighborhoods.

When purchasing salumi, choose meats that have a fresh, pearly look about them and are not too dry and hard. Avoid meats that are overspiced and oversalted. Use hot spiced meats like pepperoni as an accent, not as the centerpiece of your assortment. Have the meats sliced very thin. Once sliced, salumi dry out rapidly, so use them as soon as possible.

Serve the meats alone or with Marinated Mushrooms (page 110), Pickled Peppers (page 113), Grissini (page 162), Tuscan Bread (page 158), or any of the focaccias.

CHICKEN AND VEGETABLE SALAD WITH WALNUTS

Insalata di Pollo con le Noci

Serves 4 to 6

Homemade mayonnaise made with good olive oil is far better than the sweet-tasting stuff that comes in jars. This recipe makes about 1 cup mayonnaise, more than you will need for the salad. But you will surely find many uses for the leftover mayonnaise and it will keep well in the refrigerator for about a week. Use a relatively mild-tasting olive oil here or a combination of olive and corn oils or the flavor may be too intense.

3 carrots, 1 chopped and the remaining 2 grated

1 celery rib, chopped

1 medium onion, peeled

1 garlic clove, peeled

6 black peppercorns

Salt

1 chicken (about 3 pounds)

About ½ cup Olive Oil Mayonnaise (recipe follows)

1½ teaspoons white wine vinegar

Freshly ground black pepper

2 cups thinly sliced radicchio (about 1 medium head)

1 medium red or yellow bell pepper, cored, seeded, and finely chopped

¼ cup thinly sliced scallions

½ cup coarsely chopped toasted walnuts

Boston lettuce leaves

1. In a large pot, bring 6 quarts of water to a boil over medium heat. Add the chopped carrot, celery, onion, garlic, peppercorns, and 2 teaspoons salt. Reduce the heat to low and simmer for 30 minutes.

2. Add the chicken. Return to a simmer and cook until the chicken thigh is just tender when pierced with a fork, about 45 minutes.

3. Remove the chicken from the broth. Remove the skin and meat from the bones and cut the meat into bite-size pieces. Place the meat in a large bowl and discard the skin and bones.

4. Combine ½ cup mayonnaise and the vinegar with salt and pepper to taste.

5. Add the grated carrots, the radicchio, bell pepper, and scallions to the chicken and stir to mix. Gently stir in the mayonnaise mixture. Chill for 1 to 2 hours.

6. Just before serving, stir in the walnuts. Taste for seasoning, adding more mayonnaise or salt and pepper if desired. Serve on a platter lined with the lettuce leaves.

Olive Oil Mayonnaise

Makes about 1 cup

1 large egg, at room temperature
¾ cup extra-virgin olive oil or a combination of olive oil and corn oil
½ teaspoon Dijon mustard
¼ teaspoon salt
1 to 1½ teaspoons fresh lemon juice

In a blender jar, combine the egg, 2 tablespoons of the oil, mustard, and salt. Blend on high 10 seconds. With the machine running, add the remaining oil by droplets until the mixture is thick and smooth. Add lemon juice to taste. Cover and refrigerate.

CHICKEN IN GREEN SAUCE

Pollo in Salsa Verde

Serves 6

Salsa verde is the traditional accompaniment to *bollito misto*, a combination of beef, chicken or capon, sausages, veal, and other meats simmered for hours and served with their broth. It is not the kind of food one can indulge in often, though I make it once a year when the weather is cold. The fragrant steam from the simmering meats fills the house with warmth and delicious aromas.

But salsa verde is too good to have just once a year so I serve it over steamed vegetables, hard-cooked eggs, seafood, or poached chicken as an antipasto.

¼ **cup chopped flat-leaf parsley**
¼ **cup finely chopped drained capers**
2 tablespoons finely chopped onion
1 2-ounce can anchovy fillets, drained and chopped
2 garlic cloves, peeled and finely chopped
1 teaspoon Dijon mustard
2 tablespoons fresh lemon juice
½ **cup extra-virgin olive oil**
Salt
2 cups chicken broth
1½ pounds boned and skinned chicken breasts

1. In a bowl, whisk together the parsley, capers, onion, anchovies, garlic, mustard, and lemon juice. Stir in the olive oil and salt.

2. Cover and let stand at room temperature for 1 hour, or refrigerate for up to 1 week. Stir and taste for seasoning before using.

3. In a medium saucepan, bring the chicken broth to a simmer. Add the chicken breasts, cover, and simmer, turning once, until the chicken is just cooked through, about 5 minutes.

4. Drain the chicken and cut it into thin crosswise slices. Arrange on a platter. Drizzle with the sauce and serve.

CHICKEN SALAD WITH PINE NUTS AND RAISINS

Insalata di Pollo ai Pignoli

Serves 6 to 8

According to my husband, the flavor of pine nuts improves any salad. Apparently, the chef at Da Delfina, in Artimino, likes them too because a small portion of this pine nut—studded chicken salad is one of a series of small antipasti served at the restaurant. The sweetness of the raisins is a nice contrast to the slight bitterness of the radicchio.

2 cups chicken broth
1½ pounds boned and skinned chicken breasts
⅓ cup extra-virgin olive oil
2 tablespoons balsamic vinegar
1 tablespoon fresh lemon juice
Salt and freshly ground black pepper
⅓ cup golden raisins
4 cups thinly sliced radicchio (about 2 medium heads)
¼ cup toasted pine nuts

1. In a medium saucepan, bring the chicken broth to a simmer. Add the chicken breasts, cover, and cook, turning once, until tender, about 5 minutes.

2. Meanwhile, in a small bowl, whisk together the olive oil, vinegar, lemon juice, and salt and pepper to taste.

3. Drain the chicken and cut it into thin crosswise strips. Place the chicken and raisins in a bowl. Pour half the dressing over the chicken and toss to coat. Cover and marinate for 1 hour in the refrigerator.

4. Place the radicchio in a shallow serving bowl. Stir in the chicken mixture, then stir in the remaining dressing and the pine nuts. Serve immediately.

LIGURIAN CHICKEN SALAD

Insalata di Pollo alla Ligure

Serves 4 to 8

This salad has big chunks of moist chicken, ripe tomatoes, cucumbers, and onions, and is perfumed with fresh basil, fruity olive oil, and a hint of vinegar.

1 celery rib, chopped

1 carrot, chopped

1 medium onion, peeled

1 garlic clove, peeled

Salt

6 black peppercorns

1 chicken (about 3 pounds)

2 large ripe tomatoes, peeled, seeded, and diced

1 small cucumber, peeled and seeded

½ small red onion, peeled and thinly sliced

½ cup fresh basil leaves, torn into pieces

½ cup flat-leaf parsley, coarsely chopped

½ cup extra-virgin olive oil

3 tablespoons red wine vinegar

Pinch of dried marjoram

Freshly ground black pepper

1. In a large pot, bring 6 quarts of water to a boil. Add the celery, carrot, whole onion, garlic, 2 teaspoons salt, and the peppercorns. Simmer for 30 minutes.

2. Add the chicken. Return to a simmer and cook until the chicken thigh is just tender when pierced with a fork, about 45 minutes.

3. Remove the chicken from the broth. Remove the skin and meat from the bones and cut the meat into bite-size pieces.

4. In a large bowl, combine the chicken, tomatoes, cucumber, red onion, basil, and parsley.

5. In a small bowl, whisk together the oil, vinegar, marjoram, and salt and pepper to taste. Pour over the chicken and vegetables and toss lightly. Serve immediately.

CHICKEN WITH ARUGULA

Pollo con Arugula

Serves 6

After removing the meat from the chicken, return the bones to the pot and simmer for one hour. Cool, strain, and skim off the fat. Store in the freezer or refrigerator.

1 celery rib, chopped
1 carrot, chopped
1 medium onion, peeled
2 garlic cloves, peeled
Salt
6 black peppercorns
1 chicken (about 3 pounds)
6 anchovy fillets, finely chopped
2 teaspoons capers, drained and finely chopped
½ cup extra-virgin olive oil
2 tablespoons fresh lemon juice
1 tablespoon white wine vinegar
Freshly ground black pepper
3 bunches arugula, washed and trimmed (about 6 cups)

1. In a large pot, bring 6 quarts of water to a boil. Add the celery, carrot, onion, 1 garlic clove, 2 teaspoons salt, and the peppercorns. Simmer for 30 minutes.

2. Add the chicken. Return to a simmer and cook until the chicken thigh is just tender when pierced with a fork, about 45 minutes.

3. Remove the chicken from the broth. Remove the skin and meat from the bones and cut the meat into bite-size pieces.

4. Finely chop the remaining garlic clove. In a bowl, whisk together the garlic, anchovies, capers, olive oil, lemon juice, vinegar, and salt and pepper to taste. Pour half the dressing over the chicken.

5. Place the arugula in a shallow serving bowl and toss with the remaining dressing. Spoon the chicken into the center and serve immediately.

SWEET AND SPICY CHICKEN SALAD WITH PEPPERS

Petti di Pollo con Peperoni al Dolceforte

Serves 4 to 6

In Sicily, this warm salad is traditionally made with rabbit. It's just as delicious with chicken.

2 medium red bell peppers, cored, seeded, and cut into ½-inch-wide strips

2 tablespoons plus 2 teaspoons extra-virgin olive oil

Salt and freshly ground black pepper

1½ pounds boned and skinned chicken breasts

¾ cup fresh orange juice (about 3 juice oranges)

1 tablespoon honey

½ teaspoon crushed red pepper

2 bunches arugula, washed and trimmed (about 4 cups)

1. Preheat the oven to 400°F.

2. In a 13- × 9- × 2-inch roasting pan, toss the peppers with the 2 tablespoons oil. Sprinkle with salt and pepper. Roast, stirring occasionally, for 20 minutes.

3. Add the chicken and orange juice. Sprinkle the chicken with salt and pepper. Roast until the chicken is tender, about 15 minutes.

4. Remove the chicken and peppers and keep warm. Strain the pan juices into a small saucepan. Add the honey and red pepper. Bring to a simmer and cook for 2 minutes or until slightly reduced. Season to taste with salt and black pepper.

5. Arrange the arugula on a platter. Drizzle the remaining 2 teaspoons oil over and toss to coat. Spoon the peppers over the arugula. Cut the chicken into diagonal slices and arrange it on the vegetables. Pour the sauce over all. Serve warm.

WINE NOTES

When I was growing up, there was always a gallon jug of red wine on hand in a cool corner of our kitchen. Sometimes it was given to us by an uncle or a neighbor generous enough to share his homemade wine, but more often it was a young, fresh "burgundy" from California, the kind of rough fruity wine that left a deep purple stain on the bottom of a glass.

At dinner time, everyone drank some wine. Since milk was considered unpalatable with most foods, even the children in my family added a splash of wine to a glass of Pepsi or orange soda. Everybody drank the wine from short, fat tumblers and when the weather was warm, the adults added club soda or ice cubes. Sometimes wine was used for cooking, as a marinade for meat or fish, and in the summer wine was poured over fresh, sliced sweet peaches for dessert.

To Italians, wine is not merely a drink to be served on special occasions. Wine is considered a food and, like bread or water, no lunch or dinner would be complete without it. Unlike other beverages, wine is made to go with meals. It complements the flavors of foods, adds to one's enjoyment, and makes ordinary meals seem special.

Choosing a wine to go with antipasto is a simple matter. If you were traveling in Italy, the best wine to

Un buon bicchiere

tiene lontano

il medico.

A good glass of

wine keeps away

the doctor.

order probably would be the *vino locale*, since wines are made to go with foods from their own area. Many of these wines are available here, too, and you can select from among them the type of wine that best suits the antipasti you will be serving.

The following are descriptions of just a few of the Italian wines that go well with antipasto. The name of the region is given in small capital letters. Look for the more recent vintages.

WHITE WINE

Vino Bianco

Fiano di Avellino • CAMPAGNA •

One of my favorite white wines comes from the province of Avellino outside of Naples. It has a faint flavor of pears and hazelnuts. Producer: Mastroberardino.

Frascati • LATIUM •

Light, dry wine from the hill towns of the Castelli Romani south of Rome. The Romans drink it with all kinds of food, including the luscious *porchetta* (roast suckling pig) and often cut it with a bit of chilled *acqua minerale*. Producers: Fontana Candida, Colli Di Catone, Gotto D'Oro.

Galestro • TUSCANY •

Named for the rocky Tuscan soil, Galestro is light and lively with a pleasant fresh taste, balanced acidity, and fruit with low alcohol. Many are *frizzante*, lightly sparkling. Producers: Antinori, Castello di Gabbiano.

Gavi • PIEMONTE •

From one of Italy's finest red wine–producing regions comes this straw-colored wine with a ripe, fragrant fruit aroma and rich, full taste. Producers: Villa Banfi *Principessa*, La Chiara, Liedholm.

Greco di Tufo • CAMPAGNA •

The greco grape is a variety said to have been brought to the area by the ancient Greeks. A dry and delicate wine with a hint of bitter almonds, it goes well with grilled fish and shellfish. Producer: Mastroberardino.

Orvieto • UMBRIA •

The medieval town of Orvieto sits dramatically atop a high plateau. From the walls that surround the city, you can see the miles of vineyards that produce the grapes for this straw-yellow wine with a crisp flavor and pleasant aftertaste. Producers: Ruffino, Viselli, Antinori.

Pinot Grigio • FRIULI-VENEZIA-GIULIA AND VENETO •

Dry, delicate, and soft with a subtle nutty flavor and flinty aftertaste. Producers: Furlan, Livio Felluga, Cavit.

Soave • VENETO •

From the shores of Garda, Italy's largest lake, where the Roman poet Catullus kept his villa, this is a crisp, dry wine with a subtle flavor of apples and flowers. Producers: Bolla, Folonari, Pieropan.

Spumante Brut • VARIOUS REGIONS •

A dry, sparkling wine, not to be confused with sweet spumante, such as Asti Spumante, which is a dessert wine. Producers: Villa Banfi, Ca'del Bosco, Berlucchi.

Vernaccia di San Gimignano • TUSCANY •

From the quaint medieval hilltop town, Vernaccia is dry and fresh tasting with a slightly bitter aftertaste. Producers: Teruzzi & Puthod, San Quirico, Riccardo Falchini.

RED WINE
Vino Rosso

Barbera d'Alba • PIEMONTE •

One of Italy's best "food wines" because it has a high acid content and delicious fruity flavor that complements a wide variety of foods. I like it with cheeses, meats, stuffed vegetables, and even some fish antipasti, and it also goes well with pasta and risotto. Producers: Vietti, Giacomo Conterno, Bruno Giacosa.

Bardolino • VENETO •

A light red wine that is manufactured in large quantity by several major producers. Bardolino is refreshing and is good slightly chilled as a picnic wine. Producers: Bolla, Lamberti, Bertani.

Chianti Classico • TUSCANY •

One of my favorite red wines, Chianti has a warm, rich aroma that reminds me of sunshine on pine trees and a dry, velvety taste. Complex older vintages are superb with grilled steaks but lively young Chiantis go well with antipasti, particularly crostini, salumi, and grilled mushrooms. Producers: Viticcio, Castello di Gabbiano, Antinori.

Dolcetto d'Alba • PIEMONTE •

An intense, purple-red wine with a full, fruity flavor, Dolcetto should be drunk when it is very young—within one to three years is best. Though the name implies sweetness, Dolcetto is a dry wine. Producers: Vietti, Cogno-Marcarini, Ceretto.

Rubesco • UMBRIA •

Although the official name for this wine is Torgiano Rosso, it is familiarly called Rubesco, the name given it by the Lungarotti family, who are its most famous producers. It is a luscious, ruby-red wine with an elegant flavor. Producer: Lungarotti.

Valpolicella • VENETO •

An appealing, all-purpose wine with a medium body and rich, fruity flavor. In the hands of the right producer, Valpolicella can be excellent. Producers: Quintarelli, Masi, Bertani, Bolla.

BIBLIOGRAPHY

Alberini, Massimo. *Storia del pranzo all'Italiana*. Milan: Rizzoli, 1966.

————, and Giorgio Mistretta. *Guida all'Italia gastronomica*. Milan: Touring Club Italiano, 1984.

Artusi, Pellegrino. *La scienza in cucina e l'arte di mangiar bene*. Rome: Newton Compton, 1988.

Boni, Ada. *Il talismano della felicita*. Rome: Editore Colombo, 1972.

Bugialli, Giuliano. *Classic Techniques of Italian Cooking*. New York: Simon and Schuster, 1982.

Cavalcanti, Ottavio. *Il libro d'oro della cucina e dei vini di Calabria e basilicata*. Milan: Mursia Editore, 1979.

Da Mosto, Ranieri. *Il veneto in cucina*. Florence: Giunti-Martello, 1974.

Della Salda, Anna Gosetti. *Le ricette regionali italiane*. Milan: Solares, 1980.

Donati, Stella. *Il grande manuale della cucina regionale*. Milan: SugarCo Edizioni, S.r.l., 1982.

Field, Carol. *The Italian Baker*. New York: Harper & Row, 1985.

Gargiulo, Antonia. *Le ricette della mia cucina napoletana*. Florence: Riccio, 1984.

Grimaldi, Gianni. *Liguria in bocca*. Palermo: Il Vespro, 1979.

Hazan, Marcella. *The Classic Italian Cookbook*. New York: Knopf, 1976.

————. *More Classic Italian Cooking*. New York: Knopf, 1978.

La cucina di genova e della liguria. Genoa: Valenti Editore, 1985.

Lantermo, Alberta. *Piemonte in bocca*. Palermo: Edikronos, 1981.

Machlin, Edda Servi. *The Classic Cuisine of the Italian Jews*. New York: Everest House, 1981.

Middione, Carlo. *The Food of Southern Italy*. New York: Morrow, 1987.

Muffoletto, Anna. *The Art of Sicilian Cooking*. Garden City, N.Y.: Doubleday, 1971.

Oliver, Fiammetta di Napoli. *La grande cucina siciliana*. Milan: Moizzi Editore S.p.A., 1976.

Parenti, Giovanni Righi. *La grande cucina toscana*. Vols. 1 and 2. Milan: SugarCo Edizioni S.r.l., 1986.

Pepe, Antonietta. *Le ricette della mia cucina pugliese*. Florence: Riccio, 1981.

Romano, Franca Colonna. *Il sole ai fornelli*. Milan: Rizzoli, 1982.

Santolini, Antonella. *Umbria in bocca*. Palermo: Il Vespro, 1978.

Simeti, Mary Taylor. *Pomp and Sustenance*. New York: Knopf, 1989.

Tropea, Ivana. *Le ricette della mia cucina romana*. Florence: Riccio, 1984.

Willinger, Faith Heller. *Eating in Italy*. New York: Hearst Books, 1989.

INDEX